CHRISTIAN PATRIOTISM

··· OR ···

RELIGION AND THE STATE

ALONZO TREVIER JONES

Original publication: 1900

Due to its historical value, this study is reprinted for study by people with an interest in the final events of this earth's history.

Published by CFI Book Division

P.O. Box 159, Gordonsville, Tennessee 38563

ISBN-13: 979-8-8690-2832-7

CONTENTS

Christian Patriotism
··· or ···
Religion and the State

Introduction

Christian patriotism, loyalty to the law and government of the Most High, is the loftiest aspiration that can ever come to any soul.

THE separation of religion and the State is one of the most important questions that any people can ever be called upon to consider in connection with Christian patriotism; because the union of religion and the State has marked the greatest apostasies from God, and has caused more misery than any other thing in all history.

The complete separation of religion and the State is Christian. Unswerving loyalty to this principle is Christian patriotism. This is not a mere sentiment or side issue of Christianity; it is one of the fundamental principles and chief characteristics of Christianity.

The Bible, not merely the New Testament, but the whole Book, is the Book of Christianity. The New Testament is not a revelation new and distinct from the Old; it is the culmination of the revelation begun in the Old Testament.

The Old Testament and the New are one book—one consistent, harmonious revelation of God through Jesus Christ; because Jesus Christ is the revelation of God before the world was made, when the world was made, and through all the history of the world from beginning to end.

The first chapter of Genesis is Christian as certainly as is the first chapter of John. The book of Genesis is Christian as really as is the book of Revelation or any other book in the Bible. We repeat, therefore, that the whole Bible is the Book of Christianity, the Book of the Christian religion, the revelation of God through Jesus Christ.

And the separation of religion and the State is one of the great thoughts of this great Book. It is one of the leading principles of that Book which for man is the source of all sound principle.

Many people think that the two or three expressions of Christ as recorded in the New Testament are all that the Bible contains on the subject of the separation of Church and State; and many others are disposed even to argue against these passages, and to modify them by other passages from the Old Testament. But separation of religion and the State is one of the original thoughts of the Bible, and reaches from the beginning to the end of the Book; and neither the Book nor this subject can be fairly understood in reference to this matter till this is clearly defined in the mind.

We purpose here to give a series of studies of the Bible from beginning to end, on this great subject of Christian patriotism or the separation of religion and State.

Being one of the great thoughts of the Bible, one of the great thoughts of God and of our Lord Jesus Christ, this subject is of vital importance to men everywhere in their relations to *God*, and not merely in their relations to the State. It is a principle that is involved in the daily experience of the Christian in his relation to God; and not merely an abstract question that man can stand, as it were, apart from and view simply as a speculative question of the relations between religion and the State.

The ways of God are right. His Word is the only certain light, the only sure truth. The principles which He has announced are the only safe principles for the guidance of men. We hope, and shall seriously endeavor, to make each study so plain that every reader can easily see and readily grasp the truth of it in very principle. We shall begin at the beginning.

Chapter 1

THE FIRST OF ALL THE COMMANDMENTS

"The first of all the commandments is, Hear, O Israel, The Lord our God is one Lord; and thou shalt love the Lord thy God with all thy heart, and with all thy soul, and with all thy mind, and with all thy strength. This is the first commandment.

"And the second is like, namely this, Thou shalt love thy neighbor as thyself. There is none other commandment greater than these."

"On these two commandments hang all the law and the prophets."

THESE two commandments exist in the very nature, and circumstances of existence, of any two intelligent creatures in the universe. They existed thus in the existence of the first two intelligent creatures that ever had a place in the universe.

When the first intelligence was created and there was no creature but himself; as he owed to his Creator his existence, as he owed to God all that he was or could be, heart, soul, might, mind, and strength; it devolved upon him to render to God the tribute of all this, and to love God with all his heart, and all his soul, and all his mind, and all his strength. And this is the first of all the commandments. It is first in the very nature and existence of the first, and of every other, intelligent creature.

But the second of these would have no place if there were but one intelligent creature in the universe; for then he would have no neighbor. But when the second one was created, the first of all the commandments was *first* with him equally with the other one; and now the *second* great commandment exists in the very nature and existence of these *two* intelligent creatures, as certainly as the *first* great commandment existed in the nature and existence of the first *one*.

Each of the two created intelligences owes to the Lord all that he is or has, and all that he could ever rightly have. Neither of them has anything that is self-derived. Each owes all to God. There is between them no ground of preference. And this because of the honor which each owes to God; because to each, God is all in all. Therefore the second great commandment exists as certainly as the first; and it exists in the nature and circumstance of the very existence of intelligent creatures. Consequently, "there is none other commandment greater than these."

These two commandments, then, exist in the nature of cherubim, seraphim, angels, and men. As soon as the man was created, the first of all the commandments was there, even though there had been no other creature in the universe. And as soon as the woman was created, these two great commandments were there. And there was none other commandment greater than these.

Now, if these two great commandments had been observed by man on the earth, that is, had man never sinned, there always would have been perfect and supreme religion; *and there never would have been a State*. God would always have been by every one recognized as the only Ruler, His law as the only law, His authority as the only authority. There would have been government, but only the government of God. There would have been society, but only the society of saints. But there would have been, and could have been, no State.

Therefore it is certain that the observance of these first two of all the commandments, at any time and everywhere, which is simply Christian loyalty, means the absolute separation of religion and the State, in all who observe them. And thus the principle of separation of religion and the State inheres in the very existence of intelligent creatures.

But man did sin. And, having sinned, having departed from God, mankind did not love God with all the heart nor their neighbor as themselves. Christianity was introduced to bring man back to the position, and the original relations, which he had lost. "For we are His workmanship, created in Christ Jesus unto good works, which God hath before ordained that we should walk in them." Eph. 2:10. And Christ hath suffered for us, "the Just for the unjust, that He might bring us to God." 1 Peter 3:18.

It being, then, the one great purpose of Christianity to restore man to his original condition and relation to God, its purpose is to restore him to the condition in which he can love God with all the heart, with all the soul, with all the mind, and with all the strength, and his neighbor as himself. It is to restore him to obedience to these first two of all the commandments. It is to restore him to perfect and supreme religion.

We have seen that such a condition maintained from the beginning would have been the absolute separation of religion and the State; because, then, there never could have been any State. And now, as the one great purpose of Christianity is to restore man completely to that condition, it follows with perfect conclusiveness that Christianity in its very essence, from the beginning to the end, and everywhere, demands the absolute separation of religion and the State in all who profess it.

And it must not be forgotten that the complete separation of religion and the State in those who profess religion, can be maintained only by these persons themselves being separated from the State. For it is so plain as to be indisputable that if the professor of religion is himself a part of the State, then in *him* there is at once a union of religion and the State.

Chapter 2

The Origin of the State

IT is certain that if the two greatest of all the commandments had always been observed by all men, there never could have been a State on the earth.

There would have been society, but no State. The government would have been altogether the government of God; He, the only King, the only Governor, on earth even as in heaven.

There would have been society, but no State. Because, men loving God with all the heart, and all the soul, and all the mind, and all the strength, and their neighbors as themselves, the will of God would have been done on earth even as in heaven. All would have been one united, harmonious, happy, holy family.

There is an essential distinction between society and the State.

"Society is the union which exists between men, without distinction of frontiers—without exterior restraint—and for the sole reason that they are men.

"The *civil* society or *State* is an assemblage of men subject to a common authority, to common laws,—that is to say, a society whose members may be constrained by public force to respect their reciprocal rights. Two necessary elements enter into the idea of the State: *laws* and *force*."—Janet, *Elements of Morals*, p. 143.

This distinction, however, though clear and easily evident, is seldom recognized. Indeed, it is not recognized at all by those who are anxious to secure the union of religion and the State.

But men did not observe these two "first of all the commandments." They would not love God with all their heart; they would not love their neighbors as themselves. They rejected God as their only ruler, their only sovereign, and became ambitious to rule over one another. And thus originated politics and the State.

The Scripture outlines the story of this: "When they knew God, they glorified Him not as God, neither were thankful, but became vain in their imaginations, and their foolish heart was darkened. Professing themselves to be wise, they became fools, and changed the glory of the uncorruptible God into an image made like to corruptible man, and to birds, and four-footed beasts, and creeping things." "And even as they did not like to retain God in their knowledge, God gave them over to a reprobate mind." Rom. 1:21-25, 28.

Note that at the first men *did know God.* But they chose not to glorify Him, not to honor Him, not to give Him the first place in all their thoughts and actions. Knowing God, they did not like to retain Him in their knowledge.

The next step was that they became vain in their own imaginations. They professed themselves to be wise, *of themselves.* The consequence was that they became fools; and their foolish heart was darkened.

In their vain imaginations they made gods of their own. And then to assist themselves in their worship, they made images of the gods which they had imagined.

The image was always the outward, tangible form of the god which they had already conceived in the imagination. Imagining is simply mental *image-ing.* The outward form of the god, whether it be the shining sun in the heavens or a hideously-shaped block of wood or stone, is only the outward form of the *image*-ing that has already been performed in the *imag*ination.

Thus, from the knowledge of the true God, they went to the worship of false gods. From the light, they went into darkness. From righteousness, they went to wickedness.

This is the truth. And the records of the earliest nations witness to it. The earliest records—those of the plain of Shinar—witness that the people at first had a knowledge of the true God. The records of the next two of the earliest nations, Egypt and Assyria, bear witness to this same thing.

In all these places the earliest records testify that the gods were their first rulers and the real kings; while men, in the places of authority, were but the servants, the viceroys, of the gods who were held to be the real kings.

For instance, one of the earliest records from Shinar runs thus: "To [the god] Ninridu, his King, for the preservation of Idadu, *viceroy of Ridu*, the servant, the delight of Ninridu." Another: "To [the god] Ninip the King, *his King*, Gudea, *viceroy of* [the god] *Zirgulla*, his house built." Another: "To Nana, the lady, lady splendid, his lady, Gudea, *viceroy of Zirgulla* … raised."—*Empires of the Bible*, chap. 6, par. 3, 4.

These are not only the earliest of the records that have been *found* in that land, but they themselves show that they are of the earliest records that were *made* in that land. And they clearly testify of a time when there were no kings amongst men. The gods were the kings; and the men in authority claimed only to be the viceroys of the gods who were held to be the real kings.

And all this testifies of a time further back, when the people knew and recognized God as the only king and rightful ruler of men. They show also that this knowledge of God was so recent, and still so strong upon the minds of the people, that men who stood in places of authority had not the boldness to assume the title of king, even though they held the power.

The records of Egypt and Assyria testify precisely to these same things. And at that time, also, *there was no State*. There was society.

There came a time, however, when even this lingering knowledge of God as king and the only rightful ruler, was cut off; and the man himself assumed the full title and prerogatives of king.

The first man to do this was Nimrod. Nimrod was the first man in the world who had the boldness to take to himself the title and prerogative of king, in the face of the yet lingering idea of God as king. And the name which he bears itself testifies to the fact that his action in this was considered by men, and also by the Lord, as precisely the bold thing which is here indicated. The word "Nimrod" "signifies rebellion, supercilious contempt, and is equivalent to 'the extremely impious rebel.'"

The Bible record of Nimrod is that "he began to be a mighty one in the earth." Another translation reads: "Cush begat Nimrod, who was the first to be a despot on the earth. He was an overbearing tyrant in Jehovah's sight; wherefore the saying, Even as Nimrod, the overbearing tyrant in Jehovah's sight." Gen. 10:8, 9.

That is, Nimrod was the first one to establish the might, the power, the authority, of human government, in the form of an organized State. He was the first man to assert the power and prerogatives, and assume the title, of king over men. "And the beginning of his kingdom was Babel, and Erech, and Accad, and Calneh, in the land of Shinar."

Consequently: "With the setting up of Nimrod's kingdom, the entire ancient world entered a new historical phase. The oriental tradition which makes that warrior *the first man who wore a kingly crown*, points to a fact more significant than the assumption of a new ornament of dress, or even the conquest of a province. His reign introduced to the world a new system of relations between the governor and the governed. The authority of former rulers rested upon the feeling of kindred; and the ascendancy of the chief was an image of parental control. Nimrod, on the contrary, was a *sovereign of territory*, and of men *just so far as they were its inhabitants*, and *irrespective of personal ties*. Hitherto there had been tribes—enlarged families—*society:* now there was a nation, a political community—THE STATE. The political and social history of the world henceforth are distinct, if not divergent."—*Empires of the Bible*, chap. 6, par. 7.

Such was the true origin of the State. The State was, and is, the result of the apostasy of men from God. Such only could possibly be its origin; for if all men had always observed the two "first of all the commandments," it would have been impossible for there ever to have been any State. There could have been no human authority exercised. All would have been equally subject to God; He would have been the only sovereign.

Before Nimrod there was society. Respect of the rights of persons and of their property was maintained. It was only when the apostasy grew, and men got farther and farther from God, that the monarchical idea was established and personified in Nimrod.

Let no one misunderstand. This is not to say, nor even to imply, that there should *now* be no human government, that there should be no State, nor even that there should be no monarchy. It is simply to say that which is the truth, that if there never had been any apostasy from God, there never could have been on earth a State, nor any human government.

It is true that these things are the consequences of the apostasy from God. But men *having apostatized* from God, these things all, even to such monarchy as that of Nimrod or of Nero, became necessary, just in proportion to the degree of apostasy.

It is better that there should be a government, bad as it may be, than that there should be no government at all. Even such a government as Nimrod's or Nero's is better than none at all. But without apostasy there could never have been any human government at all; and without the apostasy having gone to a fearful length, there never could have been any *such* government as Nimrod's or Nero's.

Nimrod's example was eagerly followed by all the tribes around, until they were all absorbed in it. Society had passed away, and only States remained; and these universally idolatrous. In all that region, only Abraham believed God, even his own parents being idolaters. "They served other gods." Joshua 24:2.

God chose Abraham then to be the father of all them that believed God; the father of all who will have God alone to be their God. Abraham represented then the religion of God, the beginning of the church of God.

And from that State God separated Abraham. He said to Abraham, "Get thee out of thy country, and from thy kindred, and from thy father's house, into a land that I will show thee." Gen. 12:1.

And in thus separating Abraham from that State, from his country, God taught the people then, and through all time, the separation of religion and the State, the separation of Church and State.

And it must not be forgotten that in the case of Abraham, this universal example, the separation of religion and the State, was the separation of the *individual believer* from the State. And as Abraham was at that time the church, and he was separated from the State, in this it is plainly taught that the true separation of Church and State is in the separation of the individual church-member from the State. Besides, it is perfectly plain in itself that where the same individual is a member of the Church and of the State at the same time, there is at once *in him* a union of Church and State.

Chapter 3

THE SEPARATION OF CHURCH AND STATE

WHEN God said to Abraham, "Get thee out of thy country, and from thy kindred, and from thy father's house, unto a land that I will show thee," Abraham "went out, not knowing whither he went." Heb. 11:8.

God had not yet showed to him the land or country into which he was to go, and which was to be his. So far, the Lord had only promised to show it to him.

There were three things, however, which Abraham must do before he could fairly expect God to show him the country which He had promised, and which was to be his. First, he was to get out of his country; secondly, from his kindred; thirdly, from his father's house.

He left his country; but when he did so, his father and his kindred went with him to Haran, and dwelt there. There his father died; and now, separated from his father's house, he went on to the land of Canaan.

But there accompanied him yet one of his kindred—Lot, his brother's son. While Lot was with him, and he was thus not separated from his kindred, though separated from his country and his father's house, the time could not come for God to show to him the land, nor the country which He would give him.

But there came a day when Lot should be separated from him. Lot chose all the plain of the Jordan, and journeyed east, and "they separated thus, one from the other." Gen. 13:11.

And just then it was that God showed to Abraham the land which He had promised to show him, the country which should be his. "And the Lord said unto Abraham, *after that Lot was separated from him*, Lift up now thine eyes, and look from the place where thou art northward, and southward, and eastward, and westward; for all the land which thou seest, to thee will I give it, and to thy seed forever." Gen. 13:14, 15.

And the country which the Lord then showed to Abraham, and which He there promised him should be his for an everlasting possession—that country embraced the world; for "the promise, that he should be the heir of the world, was not to Abraham, or to his seed, through the law, but through the righteousness of faith." Rom. 4:13.

Therefore, when at the word of the Lord Abraham lifted up his eyes to see what the Lord would show him, he saw "the world to come," which is to be the everlasting possession of all them which be of faith. For "if ye be Christ's, then are ye Abraham's seed, and heirs according to the promise." Gal. 3:29.

And from that day forward Abraham "sojourned in the land of promise as in a strange country," looking for "a better country, that is, an heavenly," and looking "for a city which hath foundations, whose builder and maker is God." Heb. 11:9, 16, 8. For, though God promised that He would give to Abraham that land, and to his seed after him, yet as long as he was in this world God really "gave him none inheritance in it, no not so much as to set his foot on." Acts 7:5.

Now note: God had called Abraham out of his original country, and thus had separated him from that. Then He gave him not even so much as to set his foot on in any other country in this world.

Abraham at that time represented the religion of God. The Lord in His dealing thus with Abraham and in recording it, has shown, for all time and to all people, that it is His will that there should be an absolute separation of His religion from any State. And in thus showing the complete separation of His religion from any State, He shows that this separation consists in the separation of the individual believer of His religion, from any State. Are you walking "in the steps of that faith of our father Abraham," the friend of God? Romans 4.

Abraham, representing at that time the church of Christ, being thus totally separated by the Lord from every State and country on the earth, there is thus shown to all people, as an original truth of the Gospel of Christ, that there should be total separation of Church and State, and that the church of Christ can never have any country in the world. And in thus showing that *the church* of Christ can never have any country in this world, He shows that the *individual members* of the church of Christ can never have any country in this world; for that which composes the church of Christ is the individual membership.

So also dwelt Isaac and Jacob, heirs with Abraham of the same promise, accepting with Abraham separation from every earthly State and country, confessing "that they were strangers and pilgrims on the earth," looking for the country which God had prepared for them, and the city which hath foundations, whose builder and maker is God.

And that they accepted this freely of their own choice, by faith in God, is shown by the fact, as recorded: "Truly, if they had been mindful of that country from whence they came out, they might have had opportunity to have returned. But now they desire a better country, that is, an heavenly; wherefore God is not ashamed to be called their God, for He hath prepared for them a city." Heb. 11:15, 16.

This dealing of God with Abraham, and the record of it, were for the instruction of all the people who would believe God, from that time to the world's end. For Abraham was the called, the chosen, the friend, of God, the father of all them that believe. And all "they which be of faith are blessed with faithful Abraham." Gal. 3:9. And not the least element of instruction in this account of God's dealings with Abraham, is the great lesson it teaches that the religion of God means separation of religion and the State. Are you walking in the steps of that faith of our father Abraham? Have you gotten out of your country? Or have you still a country in this world? Is there in *you* a union of religion and the State?

Further: "Now to Abraham and his Seed were the promises made. He saith not, And to seeds, as of many; but as of one, And to thy Seed, which is Christ." Galatians 3:16. Therefore the promises recorded and referred to in the scripture, "To Abraham and his Seed," are always to Abraham and Christ, and to Abraham in Christ. And, therefore, "if ye be Christ's, then are ye Abraham's seed, and heirs according to the promise." Gal. 3:29.

And when Christ, that promised Seed, came into the world a man amongst men, then in Him, as formerly in Abraham, there was represented the religion of God and the church of Christ. And as such

He ever maintained the same principle of separation of religion and the State which He Himself had set before the world in the life and record of Abraham.

He refused to recognize, even by a sign, the wish of the people to make Him king. John 6:15. He refused, when requested, to act the part of a judge or a divider over men as to the rights of property. Luke 12:13-15. He refused to recognize the national lines of distinction, the wall of partition, which Israel in their exclusiveness had built up between themselves and other nations. He refused to judge, or to allow any others to judge, any one for not believing on Him. John 12:47, 48. He distinctly declared that, though He is a king, yet His kingdom is not of this world, and that it is not in any way connected with this world. John 18:36. He distinctly declared the separation of His religion from the State. "Render to Cæsar the things that are Cæsar's, and to God the things that are God's." Mark 12:17. And when He sent forth His disciples with His heavenly commission to preach the Gospel of His kingdom, He sent them not to one particular nation, but to "teach all nations, baptizing them in the name of the Father and the Son and the Holy Ghost." He sent them to preach the Gospel; not to one particular, favored, exclusive people, but "to every creature."

Thus it is seen again that in every phase of the fundamental principle of the religion of God and the church of Christ, from the beginning to the end of the world, there is required the absolute separation of religion and the State—the total disconnection of His church from every State and country in the world, and from the world itself.

And this total disconnection of His church from every State and country in this world, and from the world itself, is, and can be, accomplished only by the total disconnection of the individual members of His church from every State and country in the world, and from the world itself. "Ye are not of the world; for I have chosen you out of the world." "They are not of the world, even as I am not of the world." John 15:19; 17:16. Are *you?*

Chapter 4

THE RENUNCIATION OF EGYPT

IN the beginnings of Egypt the same course was followed as in the beginnings of Babylon and Assyria.

At first they knew the one true God; and He was their only King, their only Ruler.

But they did not like to retain God in their knowledge; and therefore they went into idolatry, and from idolatry into monarchy.

The Egyptian records state that the first rulers of Egypt were the gods; after them the demigods; and after these the kings.

In Egypt, however, the king was not content, as in Assyria, to call himself the viceroy of his god; he claimed to be the very embodiment of the god itself—the god was personated in the king; from him, it was declared, the people "received the breath of their nostrils;" he was "the giver of life."—*Empires of the Bible*, chap. 7, par. 38, 44.

And thus, though Nimrod was the first man to establish monarchical authority and assume the kingly title and crown, yet in Egypt his example was followed to the greatest lengths, as Egypt was undoubtedly the most idolatrous nation that ever was on the earth. There apostasy of every kind culminated, so that throughout the Bible the one word "Egypt" symbolizes everything that is contrary to God.

When the power of monarchy had filled the Mesopotamian plain, God called Abraham out of that country into the land of Canaan, where he could be free, and thus made a separation of Church and State, and preached the same to all people.

But in process of time, and by Egypt, the power of monarchy was spread over all countries, from Ethiopia to Ararat and central Asia. Then, as His people were obliged to live under the power of monarchy anyhow, the Lord put them where they could do the most possible good—He placed them at the very seat of the world's empire, in Egypt itself.

And there, through all the time of the supremacy of the Egyptian Empire, with Joseph and Moses beside the throne, and Israel amongst the people, of Egypt, God held before all nations the knowledge of Himself. And as soon as the time came when the Egyptian Empire must fall, God would place His people once more in Canaan, the pivot of the highways of the nations.

To this end there must be again taught to the world the separation of religion and the State, the separation of Church and State. God's people must be called out of Egypt, in order that they and all the nations might be instructed in the great principles of the Gospel, of supreme allegiance to God, of the separation of religion and the State, of church and country.

Moses understood this, and therefore he "refused to be called the son of Pharoah's daughter." Heb. 11:24. Moses was the adopted son of Pharaoh's daughter. Pharaoh's daughter was Pharaoh's chief wife, and queen. Moses, therefore, by the most complete claim, was heir apparent to the throne of Egypt. And as the king was then more than eighty years old, it could be but a little while till Moses would possess the throne of Egypt. The throne of Egypt was at that time the throne of the world; for the power of Egypt then ruled the world. It was the supreme State, the governing empire over all. See "*Empires of the Bible*," chapter 7.

For Moses to refuse to be called the son of Pharaoh's daughter was therefore to renounce the throne of Egypt. To renounce the throne of Egypt was to renounce the power of empire. It was definitely to disconnect from the State.

At that time Moses was called to have charge over "the house of God, which is the church of the living God." Heb. 3:2, 5; 1 Tim. 3:15. It was in obedience to this call that he renounced the throne of Egypt and the power of empire. It was because of this that he definitely disconnected himself from the State. And in recording it, God designed to teach all people that conformity to His will means the separation of Church and

State; that it means the renunciation of the throne and the power of earthly empire—the total separation of religion and the State. In recording it God designs to teach, and does teach, that union with His church means separation from the State.

And it was through the faith of Christ that Moses did all this. It was "through faith" that "Moses, when he was come to years, refused to be called the son of Pharaoh's daughter; choosing rather to suffer affliction with the people of God than to enjoy the pleasures of sin for a season; esteeming the reproach of Christ greater riches than the treasures in Egypt." Heb. 11:24-26.

Therefore, from that day to this, it has been made plain to all people that faith in God, the faith of Jesus Christ, the original principle of the Gospel and of the church, means the absolute separation of Church and State; the renunciation of the throne and power of earthly dominion; the total separation of religion and the State; and that uniting with the church of Christ means separation from the State and countries of this world.

And this is what faith in God, the faith of Jesus Christ, the fundamental principle of the Gospel and of the church, means to all people in the world to-day.

Chapter 5

THE SINGULAR NATION: CHOOSING A KING

FORTY years the Lord led and fed His people in the wilderness.

All this time He was teaching them the way of allegiance to Himself—the way of faith.

This He did in order that His purpose might be fulfilled through them in the land whither they were going to possess it.

At the end of the forty years they were encamped in the plain of Moab, opposite Jericho, preparatory to entering the land of their possession.

While there encamped, the will of God concerning them was declared by an irresistible inspiration upon the prophet Balaam, and in words of instruction to His people for all time.

And the words are these: "*Lo, the people shall dwell alone, and shall not be reckoned among the nations.*" Num. 23:9.

At that time the Lord's people composed "the church in the wilderness" (Acts 7:38); and in thus declaring that they should dwell alone and not be reckoned among the nations, He plainly declared His will that His church should be forever separated from every State and nation on the earth.

God never intended that His people should be formed into a kingdom, or State, or government, like the people of this world; nor that they should in any way be connected with any kingdom, or State, or government, of this world.

They were not to be like the nations or the people around them. They were to be separated unto God "from all the people that are upon the face of the earth." Ex. 33:16. The people were to dwell alone, and were not to be reckoned among the nations.

Their government was to be a theocracy pure and simple—God their only King, their only Ruler, their only Lawgiver. It was indeed to be a church organization, beginning with the organization of "the church in the wilderness," and was to be separated from every idea of a State. The system formed in the wilderness through Moses, was to continue in Canaan; and was intended to be perpetual.

"The government of Israel was administered in the name and by the authority of Jehovah. The work of Moses, of the seventy elders, of the rulers and judges, was simply to enforce the laws that God had given. They had no authority to legislate for the nation." For God had declared plainly, "Ye shall not add unto the word which I command you, neither shall ye diminish aught from it." Deut. 4:2.

Thus the principles of their government were solely those of a pure theocracy. And such "was and continued to be the condition of Israel's existence as a nation." In any government it is only loyalty to the principles of the government, on the part of its citizens, that can make it a success. Consequently, on the part of Israel, it was only loyalty to the principles of a pure theocracy—God their only King, their only Ruler, their only Lawgiver—that could possibly make that government a success.

But loyalty to these principles demanded that each one of the people should constantly recognize, and court, the abiding presence of God *with him* as the sole King, Ruler, and Lawgiver, in all the conduct of his daily life. Yet it is "by faith" that God dwells in the heart and rules in the life. And "without faith it is impossible to please Him." Therefore the existence of the original government of Israel, and the existence of Israel as a nation, depended upon a living, abiding faith in God, on the part of each individual of the people of Israel.

And just here, the only point where Israel could fail, Israel failed. The people did not abide in faith. They did not remain loyal to God as their King. And "Joshua the son of Nun, the servant of the Lord, died, being an hundred and ten years old. … And also all that generation were gathered unto their fathers; and there arose another generation after them, which knew not the Lord, nor yet the works which He had done for Israel." "And the children of Israel did evil in the sight of the Lord, and served Baalim; and they forsook the

Lord God of their fathers, which brought them out of the land of Egypt, and followed other gods, of the gods of the people that were round about them, and bowed themselves unto them, and provoked the Lord to anger. And they forsook the Lord, and served Baal and Ashtaroth." Judges 2:8-13.

Then all the evils that came upon them only as the result of their apostasy and idolatry, they charged back upon the government of God. In their unbelief and apostasy, they could see in the continued raids of the heathen, by which their country was sacked, and themselves were oppressed, only evidence that for all practical purposes the government of God had failed.

They therefore reached the conclusion "that in order to maintain their standing among the nations, the tribes must be united under a strong central government. As they departed from obedience to God's law, they desired to be freed from the rule of their divine Sovereign; and thus the demand for *a monarchy* became widespread throughout Israel." Accordingly, they said to Samuel, "Make us a king to judge us like all the nations." 1 Sam. 8:5.

As their hearts were fully set on having a king like all the nations, and as practically they were much like all the nations anyhow, the best thing the Lord could do for them was to let them have their king. Nevertheless, He said to Samuel, "Protest solemnly unto them." 1 Sam. 8:9.

Samuel did so, but still they insisted: "Nay; but we will have a king over us; that we also may be like all the nations; and that our king may judge us, and go out before us, and fight our battles." 1 Sam. 8:19, 20.

And of it all the Lord said to Samuel, "They have not rejected thee, but *they have rejected Me*, that I should not reign over them." And Samuel said unto them, "*Ye have this day rejected your God*," and "have said unto Him, Nay; but set a king over us." 1 Sam. 8:7; 10:19.

It was the same story of Babylon, Assyria, and Egypt, over again. When they knew God, they glorified Him not as God. And as they did not like to retain God in their knowledge, the arch-deceiver seduced them into idolatry, and from idolatry into monarchy, in order that he might gain supremacy over them, and by wordly influence entice them, or by force prohibit them, from the service of God.

It was to save them from all this that the Lord had said of them, "The people shall dwell alone, and shall not be reckoned among the nations."

If they had remained faithful to this principle, there never would have been amongst Israel a State or a kingdom.

Therefore, in announcing this principle, God intended forever that they should be completely separated from any such thing as a State or kingdom on the earth.

And as when that word was spoken they were "the church," it is absolutely certain that in announcing that principle, God intended to teach them and all people forever that His plainly-declared will is that there shall be a complete separation between His church and every State or kingdom on the earth; that there shall never be any connection between His religion and any State or kingdom in the world.

And, further: As that people were then the church, and as the Lord said they rejected Him when they formed that State and kingdom, it is perfectly plain by the Word of the Lord that whenever the church forms any connection with any State or kingdom on the earth, in the very doing of it she rejects God.

But it is impossible for the church ever to form any connection with any State except by the *individual members* of the church forming a connection with the State. Therefore, as the church in forming such connection rejects God, and as it is impossible to do this except by the individual members of the church, it is perfectly plain that the teaching of the Word of God is that for members of the church to form connection with the State is to reject God.

And from ancient time all this was written for the admonition of those upon whom the ends of the world are come. Will the people to-day be admonished by it?

Chapter 6

"Like All the Nations"

God had said of Israel, "Lo, the people shall dwell alone, and shall not be reckoned among the nations." Num. 25:9.

But, contrary to His expressed will, and against His solemn protest, Israel set up a kingdom and established a State.

They did this, they plainly said, that they might be "like all the nations." Contrary to all the Lord's wishes, the people would "be reckoned among the nations."

But Israel was the church, while all the nations were States. Israel, therefore, could not be like the nations without forming themselves into a State.

But Israel, being the church, could not possibly from themselves into a State without at the same time, and in the very doing of it, forming a union of Church and State.

They did form themselves into a State, and did thus unite Church and State. But as this was contrary to the Lord's plain Word, and against His solemn protest, it certainly stands as the truth that any union of Church and State is against the plain Word and the solemn protest of God.

Israel as "the church," which is "the pillar and ground of the truth," was the depository and the representative of the true religion in the world. Then when Israel formed themselves into a State, this was nothing else than a union of *religion* and the State. And as their forming of a State was contrary to the expressed will and the solemn protest of the Lord, it is clearly the truth that any connection between religion—and above all the true religion—and the State is positively against the expressed will and the solemn protest of God.

And as Israel, the depository and representative of the true religion, in order to form a union of religion and the State, had to reject

God, it is certainly true that every other people, in forming a union of religion and the State, do, in the very doing of it, reject God.

Nothing can be plainer, therefore, than that the God of heaven and earth, the God and Father of our Lord Jesus Christ, is eternally opposed to a union of religion and the State. He will never be a party to any such transaction.

This is why He desired that "the people should dwell alone." This is why He would have it that they should "not be reckoned among the nations." He desired that they should abide with Him, and have Him their only God, their only King, their only Ruler, their only Lawgiver—their "all in all."

God wanted not only that Israel, but that all people on the earth, should know that He is better than all other gods, that He is a better King than all other kings, that He is a better Ruler than all other rulers, that He is a better Lawgiver than all other lawgivers, that His law is better than all other laws, and that His government is better than all other governments.

For this reason He would station Israel in Palestine, at the pivot of the highways of the nations; with the God of heaven as their only King, Ruler, and Lawgiver; with His law their only law, and His government their only government; the people dwelling alone and not reckoned among the nations—a holy, happy people; a glorious church.

Dwelling thus in the sight of all the nations that had forgotten God, those nations would be constantly taught the goodness of God and would be once more drawn to Him. Accordingly He told them: "Behold I have taught you statutes and judgments, ... that ye should do so in the land whither ye go to possess it. Keep therefore and do them; for this is your wisdom and your understanding in the sight of the nations, which shall hear all these statutes, and say, Surely this great nation is a wise and understanding people." Deut. 4:5, 6.

But Israel would not have it so. Israel would "be reckoned among the nations." Israel would be "like all the nations." And so it has been, from that day to this. God has never been allowed by His professed people to reveal Himself to the world as He really is. His church has always been too willing to "be reckoned among the nations," too willing to be "like all the nations." She has always been too willing to be joined to the State, to be a part of the State, to have religion a matter of State and government, "like all the nations." And so it is with the church in all the world to-day.

"'Like all the nations.' The Israelites did not realize that to be in this respect *unlike* other nations was a special privilege and blessing. God had separated the Israelites from every other people, to make them His own peculiar treasure. But they, disregarding this high honor, eagerly desired to imitate the example of the heathen.

"And still the longing to conform to wordly customs and practices exists among the professed people of God. As they *depart from the Lord* they become ambitious for the gains and honors of the world. Christians are constantly seeking to imitate the practices of those who worship the god of this world. Many urge that by uniting with worldlings and conforming to their customs, they might exert a stronger influence over the ungodly.

"But all who pursue this course thereby separate from the Source of their strength. Becoming the friends of the world, they are the enemies of God. For the sake of earthly distinction they sacrifice the unspeakable honor to which God has called them, of showing forth the praises of Him who hath called us out of darkness into His marvelous light.

"The days of Israel's greatest prosperity were those in which they acknowledged Jehovah as their King—when the laws and government which He established were regarded as superior to those of all other nations."—*Patriarchs and Prophets*, chap. 59, par. 8-13. And such will be the days of any people's greatest prosperity.

God's laws, just as they stand, without any re-enactment, without any adding to or diminishing from, are superior to all other laws. His government, administered by Himself through the operation of His own eternal Spirit in each individual heart, is superior to every other government.

But how shall the people know this, who know not God, so long as *His own people* will not have it so? How shall the nations know this, when His own professed church will not recognize it nor have it so?

Instead of holding fast God's laws and government as superior to those of all States and nations, the professed people of God consider that they must enter the politics and shape the policies, that they must tinker the laws and manipulate the governments, of the States and nations of the world.

Instead of magnifying God's laws and government before all the world, as superior to the laws and governments of all the nations, and showing unswerving allegiance to them as such, the people of the professed churches of God seek to mingle heavenly citizenship with earthly citizenship; and to bring down from their superior place the laws and government of God, and mix them up with the laws and government of all the nations in an unseemly and ungodly union of religion and the State.

And thus the people of the professed churches of God, of the young people's societies and leagues professing Christianity—of all the combined church elements of the land—are following directly in the track of the church of ancient Israel; they will not dwell alone; they will be reckoned among the nations; they will be like all the nations; they will join themselves to the State; they will form a union of religion and the State; they will reject God, that He should not reign over them.

RESULT OF BEING "LIKE THE NATIONS"

ISRAEL would form a State, and have a king, that they might be "like all the nations."

All the nations were heathen. To be "like all the nations," then, was only to be like the heathen.

All the nations became heathen by rejecting God. Then when Israel would be "like all the nations"—like all the heathen,—they could do so only by rejecting God.

It was therefore but the simple statement of a fact when the Lord said, "They have rejected Me, that I should not reign over them."

When Israel formed a State, they thereby created a union of religion and the State. But they had to reject God in order to form a State. Therefore they had to reject God in order to form a union of religion and the State.

It follows, therefore, plainly, that no people can ever form a union of religion and the State without rejecting God.

But though Israel had rejected God, yet He did not reject them. He still cared for them; and, through His prophets, still sought to teach and guide them, ever doing His best to save them from the evil consequences which were inevitable in the course which they had taken.

Long before the days of Samuel and Saul, Israel had been taught what would be the outcome of forming themselves into a State and choosing a king; for the formation of a kingdom in the days of Saul was but the culmination of a long-cherished desire in that direction.

After the great victories of Gideon, a hundred years before the day of Saul, "the men of Israel said unto Gideon, Rule thou over us, both thou, and thy son, and thy son's son also; for thou hast delivered us from the hand of Midian." Judges 8:22.

This was nothing else than a proposition to establish at that time a kingdom, with Gideon as the first king, and the kingship to be hereditary in his family. But Gideon refused the offer, and "said unto them, I will not rule over you; neither shall my son rule over you; *the Lord shall rule over you.*"

Gideon knew that such a proposition meant the rejection of God; and he would have no part in any such thing. But the desire still lurked among the people; and forty years afterward, upon the death of Gideon, it was manifested openly in the men of Shechem making Abimelech, a son of Gideon, king in Shechem.

But in a parable, Jotham, the only son of Gideon who had survived the slaughter wrought by Abimelech, mapped out plainly to the people what would be the sure result of their venture.

Jotham stood on the top of Gerizim and called to the people of Shechem, and said:—

"The trees went forth on a time to anoint a king over them; and they said unto the olive tree, Reign thou over us. But the olive tree said unto them, Should I leave my fatness, wherewith by me they honor God and man, and go to be promoted over the trees? And the trees said to the fig tree, Come thou, and reign over us. But the fig tree said unto them, Should I forsake my sweetness, and my good fruit, and go to be promoted over the trees? Then said the trees unto the vine, Come thou, and reign over us. And the vine said unto them, Should I leave my wine, which cheereth God and man, and go to be promoted over the trees? Then said all the trees unto the bramble, Come thou, and reign over us. And the bramble said unto the trees, If in truth you anoint me king over you, then come and put your trust in my shadow; and if not, let fire come out of the bramble, and devour the cedars of Lebanon. Now therefore, if ye have done truly and sincerely, in that ye have make Abimelech king, ...then rejoice ye in Abimelech, and let him also rejoice in you; but if not, let fire come out from Abimelech, and devour the men of Shechem, and the house of Millo; and let fire come out from the men of Shechem, and from the house of Millo, and devour Abimelech." Judges 9:8-20.

And so it came to pass; for in three years the distrust and dissension had so grown between the parties to the transaction respecting the kingship, that open war broke out, which ended only with the death of Abimelech; and, with that, the end of their experiment at setting up a kingdom.

Now all this was held up before all Israel who should come after, as a solemn warning and a forcible admonition of what would inevitably be the result of any attempt at setting up a kingdom. And when, in disregard of all this, and against the Lord's open protest, they did at last again set up a kingdom, this very result, though longer delayed, did inevitably come.

Almost all the reign of Saul, their first king, was spent by him in envy and jealousy of David and a steady seeking to kill him. The reign of David was marred by his own great sin, which he never could have carried out if he had not been king; and was also disturbed by the treason of his chief counselor, and the insurrection of his son Absalom. The latter half of the reign of Solomon was marked by his great apostasy, and was cursed by the abominable idolatries that came in with his heathen wives—all "princesses," the daughters of kings—and which in turn brought heavy burdens and oppression upon the people.

At the end of the reign of these three kings, the nation had been brought to a condition in which it was not well that they should continue as one; and they were therefore divided into two—the Ten Tribes forming the kingdom of Israel, and the two other tribes forming the kingdom of Judah.

And from that day, with the Ten Tribes there was continuous course of apostasy, of contention, and of regicide, till at last, from the terrors of anarchy, they were compelled to cry out, "We have no king." Hosea 10:3. Then the Lord offered Himself to them again, saying: "Thou hast fled from Me." "O Israel, thou hast destroyed thyself." "Return unto Me." "I will be thy King." Hosea 7:13; 13:9, 10. But they would not return, and consequently were carried captive to Assyria, and were scattered and lost forever.

When this happened to the kingdom of Israel, it could yet be said of Judah, "Judah yet ruleth with God, and is faithful with the saints." Hosea 11:12. But this was only for a little while. Judah, too, went steadily step by step downward in the course of apostasy, until of her too the word had to be given: "*Remove the diadem, take off the crown; ...* exalt him that is low, and abase him that is high. I will overturn, overturn, overturn it; and *it shall be no more*, until He come whose right it is, and I will give it Him." Eze. 21:25-27.

Thus Judah too was obliged to say, We have no king. And Judah had to go captive to Babylon, with her city and temple destroyed, and the land left desolate. Thereafter the Lord was obliged to govern His people by the heathen powers, until He Himself should come. And even when He came, because He would not at once set Himself up as a worldly king and sanction their political aspirations, they refused to recognize Him at all. And when at last even Pilate appealed to them, "Shall I crucify your King?" they still, as in the days of Samuel, insisted on rejecting God, and cried out, "We have no king but Cæsar." John 19:15.

And this was but the direct outcome, and the inevitable logic, of the step that they took in the days of Samuel. When they rejected God and *chose Saul,* in that was wrapped up the rejection of the Lord and their choosing *of Cæsar.* In rejecting God that they might be like all the nations, they became like all the nations that rejected God.

And such was the clear result of the union of Church and State among the people of Israel. And it is all written precisely as it was worked out in detail, for the instruction and warning of all people who should come after, and for the admonition of those upon whom the ends of the world are come.

Will the professed people of God to-day in the churches, societies, leagues, unions, and associations of all sorts, everywhere, learn the lesson taught thus in the Word of God of the experience of the people of God of old who would have a State, and so rejected God?

Chapter 8

THE TRUE PRINCIPLE TAUGHT TO BABYLON

GOD had delivered His people from Egypt, and had united them to Himself in order that they might be separated from all the nations. And having brought them out of Egypt, and joined them to Himself, He said of them, "The people shall dwell alone and shall not be reckoned among the nations." Num. 23:9. It was only by remaining faithful to their union with God that they could be separated from all the nations. Ex. 33:16.

Israel was then the church,—"the church in the wilderness." Acts 7:38. That church was united to God in solemn covenant, upon which the Lord said, "I am married unto you," and, "I was an husband unto them." Thus was that church united to God. And in this there was the complete separation of Church and State.

But Israel was unfaithful to God. She rejected Him and set up a State, and thus formed a union of Church and State. The result was the complete ruin of the State which they had formed; the scattering of the people in captivity among the nations; and the desolation of their land. In their captivity and their trouble they sought the Lord in contrition; and joined themselves again in faithfulness to Him. And this brought them back to their original position of being the church only, and so to their original condition of total separation of Church and State.

God had planted Israel—His church—in Canaan to be the light of the world, to give the knowledge of the true God; as at that time and for ages afterward Palestine was the pivot of the known world. By their being faithful to Him and having Him abide with them, He intended that they should influence all the nations for good. But they revolted and became not only "like all the nations," but even "worse than the heathen." Therefore the land became sick of them, and spewed them out, as it had spewed out the heathen before them. Lev. 18:25, 28; 20:22.

As by their apostasy and union of Church and State, Israel had frustrated God's purpose to enlighten all nations by them in the land where He had planted them, He would fulfill His purpose, nevertheless; and, separating them again entirely from the State, would enlighten all the nations by them in the lands where He had scattered them. Israel, by becoming like all the nations, had lost the power to arrest and command the attention of all the nations, that the nations might know God, and be taught of Him. Nevertheless, God would now use them to enlighten those who, under Him, had *acquired* the power to arrest and command the attention of all the nations. Thus *by them* still He would bring to all the nations the knowledge of the true God, and teach them that "the Most High ruleth in the kingdom of men, and giveth it to whomsoever He will." Dan. 4:17. This is the whole philosophy of the captivity and subjection of Israel and Judah to Assyria, Babylon, Medo-Persia, Grecia, and Rome.

God conveyed to the kings and people of these mighty empires, the knowledge of Himself and of His truth for people and kings. And, as we have found over and over in these studies that the separation of religion and the State is one of the fundamental principles of the truth of God for kings and nations, this is one of the great truths taught to the kings and people of these great empires. And this instruction was written out in the Word of God for the instruction of all kings and people until the world's end.

In the second year of his reign alone, to King Nebuchadnezzar there was shown in a dream a great image, whose head was of gold, his breast and arms of silver, his sides of brass, his legs of iron, and his feet and toes part of iron and part of clay. By the word of the Lord through Daniel this was explained to Nebuchadnezzar as signifying the course of empire from that time until the end of the world.

This dream was given to Nebuchadnezzar because that, while upon his bed, thoughts had come into his mind as to "what should come to pass hereafter." From what came to pass afterward *with him*, it is evident that his thoughts upon that question were to the effect that the mighty kingdom of Babylon, which *he* ruled—the head of gold—would in its greatness and glory continue on and on indefinitely. To correct this view, and to show him the truth, was the purpose of the dream.

The instruction in the dream, through the divine interpretation, was that the golden glory of his kingdom would continue but a little while, and then another would arise, inferior to his, and another, and another, and then there would be division, with all these descending in a regular scale of inferiority; and then, at last, "the God of heaven" would "set up a kingdom," and *this alone* would be the kingdom that should stand forever, and not be given to other people.

But Nebuchadnezzar would not accept this view of the subject. Accordingly, he formulated his own idea in a great image, about a hundred feet tall, *all* of gold from head to feet. This image he set up in the plain of Dura, in the province of Babylon, to be worshiped, and called all his princes, governors, sheriffs, captains, rulers of the provinces, and people generally, to worship it.

This was a positive setting up of his own idea against that of God. This was to declare to all people that *his* golden kingdom was to endure forever; that there was to be no such thing as another kingdom arising separate from his and inferior to it, and after that others, descending so low as iron mixed with miry clay. No! there should be only his golden kingdom of Babylon, and it should never be broken nor interrupted; but should stand forever.

In a number of points this was an open challenge to the Lord. It was the assertion that Nebuchadnezzar's idea of the kingdoms of men should be accepted as the true and divine idea, as against that of God's, which had been given. It was the assertion that the embodiment of this opposing idea should be worshiped as God. As the idea and the embodiment of it was altogether Nebuchadnezzar's, this was simply the putting of Nebuchadnezzar himself in the place of God, as the ruler in the kingdom of men, the head of all religion, and the director of all worship.

A great day was set for the dedication of Nebuchadnezzar's idea, and the inauguration of the universal worship of it. A great multitude was assembled of many peoples, nations, and languages of his wide realm. When all were assembled, a herald proclaimed: "To you it is commanded, O people, nations, and languages, That at what time ye hear the sound of the cornet, flute, harp, sackbut, psaltery, dulcimer, and all kinds of music, ye fall down and worship the golden image that Nebuchadnezzar the king hath set up: and whoso falleth not down and worshippeth shall the same hour be cast into the midst of a burning fiery furnace."

In the great assembly were three young Jews—Shadrach, Meshach, and Abed-nego. And when all the others fell down and worshiped, these stood bolt upright, paying no attention to the law that had just then been proclaimed, nor to the image. They were at once reported and accused to the king. Then the king "in his rage and fury" commanded them to be brought before him. It was done. He asked them if it was true and of purpose that they had not worshiped. He then repeated his decree and the dreadful penalty. But they answered: "O Nebuchadnezzar, we are not careful to answer thee in this matter. If it be so, our God whom we serve is able to deliver us from the burning fiery furnace, and He will deliver us out of thine hands, O king. But if not, *be it known unto thee*, O king, that *we will not serve thy gods, nor worship the golden image which thou hast set up.*"

The furnace was heated seven times hotter than usual, and they were bound and cast into it. But suddenly the king rose up in astonishment from his throne and cried to his counselors, "Did not we cast *three* men *bound* into the midst of the fire? They answered and said unto the king, True, O king." But he exclaimed, "Lo, I see *four* men *loose*, walking in the midst of the fire, and they have no hurt; and the form of the fourth is like the Son of God."

Then the king called them forth, and said in the presence of all: "Blessed be the God of Shadrach, Meshach, and Abed-nego, who hath sent His angel, and delivered His servants that trusted in Him, and *have changed the king's word*, and yielded their bodies, that they might not serve nor worship any god, except their own God."

God had commanded all nations to serve King Nebuchadnezzar, and that whatsoever nation would not serve him, that nation the Lord would punish. Yet here He wrought a wondrous miracle to deliver the men who had openly and directly refused to obey a plain and direct command of the king. How could this consistently be?—Easily enough. This command, this law, of the king was wrong. He was demanding a service which he had no right to require. In making him king of the nations, the Lord had not made him king *in the religion* of the nations. In making him the head of all the nations. God had not made him the head of *religion*.

But being an idolater, and having grown up amid idolatrous systems, Nebuchadnezzar did not know this. With idolaters, religion always has been, and still is, a part of the government. In heathen systems, religion and the governments are always united; while in the true system, the genuine Christian system, they are always separate.

And this was the lesson which God there taught to Nebuchadnezzar. In a way in which it was impossible not to understand, the Lord showed to that king that he had nothing whatever to do with the religion, nor with the directing of the worship, of the people. The Lord had brought all nations into subjection to King Nebuchadnezzar as to their *bodily* service; but now, by an unmistakable evidence, this same Lord showed to King Nebuchadnezzar that He had given him no power nor jurisdiction whatever in their *souls'* service.

The Lord thus showed to King Nebuchadnezzar that, while in all things between nation and nation, or man and man, all people, nations, and languages had been given to him to serve him, and he had been made ruler over them all; yet in things between men and God, the king was plainly and forcibly given to understand that he had nothing whatever to do. The God of heaven there taught to that king, and through him to all kings, rulers, and people forever, that in all matters of religion and worship, in the presence of the rights of conscience of *the individual*, the word of the king *must change;* the decree of the ruler *is naught*.

And this was written for our admonition upon whom the ends of the world are come. This is important instruction and present truth to-day. For throughout the whole English-speaking world *to-day* King Nebuchadnezzar's example of arrogance is being followed—and that even by those who profess to know God and to be guided by the Bible. Nebuchadnezzar's offense was in setting up his own idea and forming it into a decree and then enforcing it as the law. And throughout these nations to-day, there are people who profess to know God and to be guided by the Bible, who have set up their own or some other one's altogether human idea of the Sabbath against God's idea of the Sabbath-Sunday against the Sabbath of the Lord—and have secured the framing of it into a decree, and are having it enforced as the law. But it is all wrong, just as Nebuchadnezzar's assumption was wrong. And every one who will be faithful to God must say, We will not serve thy gods nor worship the image of the Sabbath which thou hast set up. And in the presence of the rights of conscience of the individual to-day, the word of the ruler must change; such laws are simply naught.

Nebuchadnezzar learned his lesson. And this truth was spread to all the nations and languages in that day; and it must be spread to all in *this* day. Will all who to-day are following his wrong course, learn this lesson and correct their ways, as did he?

Chapter 9

THE TRUE PRINCIPLE TAUGHT TO MEDO-PERSIA

THE night in which Babylon fell Daniel had been appointed by King Belshazzar "the third ruler in the kingdom," because of his interpretation of the terrible handwriting on the wall. The reason that the highest honor that could be bestowed on him was that of *third* ruler was that Belshazzar was only associate king with his father. This gave two kings, and so a first and second ruler; and another could not be higher than *third* ruler.

Thus it was with Daniel; and when that same night Babylon fell, Belshazzar was slain, and his father was a prisoner, and no longer king; this left Daniel the chief official, with whom the conquerors could communicate in rearranging the affairs of the Babylonian State. Because of this, and more particularly "because an excellent spirit was in him," the king of conquering Media and Persia thought to set him over "the whole realm." Thus "this Daniel was preferred above the presidents and princes."

When all the other presidents, princes, governors, and captains saw that Daniel, a captive Jew, was preferred before themselves, who were high and mighty Medes and Persians, they were much dissatisfied. And when they discovered that he was likely to be yet further promoted, they determined to break him down utterly. Therefore they formed a conspiracy, and diligently "sought to find occasion against Daniel concerning the kingdom."

But with all their diligence, and with all their suspicions and prejudiced care, "they could find none occasion nor fault; forasmuch as he was faithful, neither was there any error or fault found in him." There was, however, one last resource, which, by a trick, they might employ. They knew that he feared God. They knew that his service to the Lord was actuated by such firm principle that, in rendering that service, he would not dodge, nor compromise, nor swerve a hair's breadth, upon any issue that might be raised.

"Then said these men, We shall not find any occasion against this Daniel, except we find it against him concerning the law of his God." But even in this there was nothing upon which they might "*find*" an "occasion." In order to find it they must *create* it; and create it they did. Pretending to be great lovers of their king and country, and to have much and sincere concern for the honor of the king and the preservation of the State, "they assembled together to the king," and proposed "to establish a royal statute, and to make a firm decree," that whosoever should ask any petition of any god or man for thirty days, save of King Darius, should be cast into the den of lions. They presented the case in such a plausible way, and with such evident care for the public good, that Darius was completely hoodwinked, and "signed the writing and the decree." Thus the invention of the conspirators became "the law of the land."

Daniel knew that the writing was signed. He knew that it was now the law—the law of the Medes and Persians too, which could not be altered. Yet, knowing this, "he went into his house" and "kneeled upon his knees three times a day, and prayed, and gave thanks before his God, *as he did aforetime*." He knew perfectly that no law of the Medes and Persians, nor of any other earthly power, could ever, of right, have anything to say or do with any man's service to God. He went on just as aforetime, because, practically, and in principle, all things were just as aforetime. So far as concerned the conduct of the man who feared God, any law on that subject was no more than no law at all on that subject.

In the Medes and Persians a new set of men had come upon the world's stage; the power of empire had passed into new hands. And these new rulers, as well as Nebuchadnezzar, must be taught the truth of the separation of religion and the State. And in order that they should have opportunity to learn this, Daniel, who was the possessor and representative of this great truth, must stand, unswervingly, to the principle. And so he did.

"Then these men assembled, and found Daniel praying and making supplication before his God." They expected to find him praying; that was exactly what they "assembled" for. And Daniel *was not afraid* that they would find him doing so. They immediately hurried away to the king, and asked him, "Hast thou not signed a decree, that every man that shall ask a petition of any god or man within thirty days, save of thee, O king, shall be cast into the den of lions? The king answered and said. The thing is true, according to the law of the Medes and Persians, which altereth not. Then answered they and said before the king, That Daniel, which is of the children of the captivity of Judah, regardeth not thee, O king, nor the decree that thou hast signed, but maketh his petition three times a day."

Then the king suddenly awoke to the fact that he had been duped. And "he was sore displeased with himself, and set his heart on Daniel to deliver him; and he labored till the going down of the sun to deliver him." But it was all of no avail; the conspirators were persistent to frustrate every effort which the king could make. And they had a ready and conclusive argument against everything that might be proposed. That argument was "the law:" "Know, O king, that the law of the Medes and Persians is, That no decree nor statute which the king establisheth may be changed." There was no remedy; the law must be enforced. Accordingly, though most reluctantly, "the king commanded, and they brought Daniel, and cast him into the den of lions."

The king passed the night in fasting and sleeplessness, and very early in the morning went in haste to the den of lions, and "cried with a lamentable voice, … O Daniel, servant of the living God, is thy God, whom thou servest continually, able to deliver thee from the lions?" To the infinite delight of the king, Daniel answered: "O king, live forever. My God hath sent His angel, and hath shut the lions' mouths, that they have not hurt me; forasmuch as *before Him* INNOCENCY was found in me; and also *before thee*, O king, have I done *no hurt*."

That is divine testimony, published to all the world, that innocence before God is found in the man who disregards any human law that interferes with his service to God. It is also divine testimony that the man who disregards such laws, in so doing does "no hurt" to the king, to the State, nor to society.

Thus God taught to the rulers of the Medo-Persian Empire the separation of religion and the State; that with men's relationship to God, rulers and States can have nothing whatever to do. And it was written for the instruction of all rulers and States unto the world's end.

In these two experiences recorded in the book of Daniel—the one of Nebuchadnezzar and the worship of his great golden image, the other of the conspirators against Daniel's service to God—all people are taught in the most impressive way, that the God of heaven forbids any ruler to require His subjects to conform to His ideas in religion, and forbids all people to frame any law on any subject touching men's relation to God. In these two experiences the God of heaven, in the strongest possible way, teaches all people, and particularly *His own people*, that in the presence of the rights of conscience, in the presence of men's relationship to God, and in all matters of religion, the word and authority of every king or ruler must give way; that all laws framed, which touch in any manner men's relationship to God, which touch any matter of religious observance, are simply *naught*— are no more than no law at all on such subject. In it all, the God of heaven also teaches to all that He vindicates and *declares innocent* all who refuse obedience to such decrees of kings and rulers, all who utterly disregard all such laws; and also certifies to all kings, rulers, and people that those who do disregard all such laws do "*no hurt*" to either king, ruler, or people.

And these lessons need to be perseveringly taught everywhere today. In almost every country in the world, and especially in the English-speaking countries, the schemes and inventions of men in matters religious, and particularly as to the observance of Sunday, are crowded into the law and so forced upon all the people. These men profess to be jealous guardians of religious liberty and the rights of conscience. They "do not believe in enforcing religion upon anybody." Yet all the time they are steadily working to get religious dogmas and institutions recognized and fixed in the law, and then demand *obedience to the law*, and throw upon the dissenter the odium of "lawlessness, and disrespect for constituted authority," while they pose as the champions of "law and order," the "conservators of the State, and the stay of society;" exactly as did the conspirators against Daniel.

Sunday, not only according to their own showing, but by every other fair showing that can be made, is a religious institution, a church affair, only. This they all know. And yet, in almost every land, those people are working constantly to get this church institution fixed, and more firmly fixed, *in the law*, with penalties attached that are more worthy of barbarism than of civilization; and then, when anybody objects to the enforcement of such laws, they all cry out: "It is not a question of religion at all; religion hasn't anything to do with it; it is simply a question of regard for law. The law! The law! It is the law of the land! We are not asking any religious observance by anybody; all that we ask is *respect for the law!*" But the lessons in the book of Daniel teach to all people that no religious or ecclesiastical institution or rite has *any right to any place in the law*. And that when against right it is put into the law, it gains no force whatever from that, and is to receive no respect nor recognition whatever.

And thus by the word and work of God in the book of Daniel, there is taught to all kings and all people unto the end of the world, the total separation of religion and the State.

Chapter 10

CHRIST THE EXAMPLE

Jesus Christ came into the world to bring to men the true knowledge of God; for "God was in Christ reconciling the world unto Himself." 2 Cor. 5:19. He came to reveal to men the kingdom of God,—to enunciate its principles, to manifest its spirit, to reveal its character. Of it He said: "My kingdom is not of this world." John 18:36. "Except a man be born again, he can not see the kingdom of God." John 3:3. And His apostles declared, "The kingdom of God is … righteousness and peace and joy in the Holy Ghost." Rom. 14:17.

"My kingdom is not of this world." Every kingdom, every State, every government of men, is altogether of this world and of this world alone. How then can anybody be of any earthly kingdom or State and of the kingdom of God at the same time? Those who are of the church are of the kingdom of God, because the church is the church of God, and not of this world—it is composed of those who are "chosen out of the world." Those who are of the State are of this world, because the State is altogether and only of this world.

And, indeed, were not "*all* the kingdoms of the world and the glory of them" offered to Jesus for His very own? Why did He not take them and rule over them and convert them and thus save them—He *could* not, because to have taken them would have been to recognize "the god of this world," by whom they were offered. Luke 4:5-8. And so is ever, the kingdom of this world is offered ever only by Satan; and all who are Christ's will refuse it, as did our Example, and as did Moses, His chosen forerunner and type.

Christ was and is the embodiment of the church and of all Christianity. Therefore, and thus, in the Word of Christ, in the very principles of the cause of Christ, there is taught the separation of Church—of Christianity—and State as complete and as wide as in the separation between the kingdom of God and the kingdoms of this world; and that is as complete and as wide as is the separation between God and this world.

Accordingly, Christ says in another place, "Render therefore unto Cæsar the things which are Cæsar's and unto God the things that are God's." Matt. 22:21. In that time the head of the Roman Empire, the personification of the world's power, was Cæsar. And in that Roman world-system it was claimed that whatsoever was Cæsar's was God's; because to all the people of that world-system Cæsar was God. He was set before the people as God; the people were required to worship him as God; incense was offered to his image as to God. In that system the State was divine, and Cæsar was the State. Therefore that system was essentially a union of religion and the State.

In view of this, when Jesus said, "Render therefore unto Cæsar the things which are Cæsar's; and unto God the things that are God's," He denied to Cæsar, and so to the State, every attribute, or even claim, of divinity. He showed that another than Cæsar is God. Thus He entirely separated Cæsar and God. He entirely separated between the things which are due to Cæsar and those which are due to God. The things that are due to Cæsar are not to be rendered to God. The things due to God are not to be rendered to Cæsar. These are two distinct realms, two distinct personages, and two distinct fields of duty. Therefore, in these words Jesus taught as plainly as it is possible to do, the complete separation of religion and the State; that no State can ever rightly require anything that is due to God; and that when it is required by the State, it is not to be rendered.

Again: Jesus is the Example whom God has set to be the Guide to every person in this world in every step that can be taken in the right way. Any step taken by anybody in a way in which the Lord Jesus did not go is taken in the wrong way. He hath left us "an example, that ye should follow His steps." 1 Peter 2:21. Whosoever saith that he "abideth in Him ought himself also so to walk, even as He walked." 1 John 2:6. And Jesus never, in any manner nor to any degree, took any part in political matters nor in any affairs of the State. Jesus was then, and is forever, the embodiment of true religion. Therefore, in His whole life's conduct of absolute separation from everything political, from all affairs of the State, there is taught to all the world, and especially to all believers in Him, the complete separation of the religion of Christ, and of all who hold it, from everything political and from all affairs of the State.

So faithfully did He hold to that principle that when a man asked Him only, "Speak to my brother, that he divide the inheritance with me," He refused, with the words, "Man, who made Me a judge or a divider over you?" and then said to them all, "Take heed and beware of covetousness; for a man's life consisteth not in the abundance of the things which he possesseth." Luke 12:13-15. Oh, if only all who have professed to be His followers had held aloof from all affairs of politics and the State, how vastly different would have been the history of the Christian era! What a blessing it would have been to the world! What floods of misery and woe mankind would have been spared!

And why was it that Jesus thus persistently kept aloof from all affairs of politics and the State? Was it because all things political, judicial, and governmental were conducted with such perfect propriety, and with such evident justice, that there was no place for anything better, no room for improvement such as even He might suggest?—Not by any means. Never was there more political corruption, greater perversion of justice, and essential all-pervasive evil of administration, than at that time. Why, then, did not Jesus call for "municipal reform"? Why did He not organize a "Law and Order League"? Why did He not disguise Himself and make tours of the dives and the gambling-dens, and entrap victims into violation of the law? And why did He not employ other spies to do the same, in order to get against the representatives of the law evidence of maladministration by which to arraign them and to compel them to enforce the law, and thus reform the city, regenerate society, and save the State, and so establish the kingdom of God? Why? The people were ready to do anything of that kind that might be suggested. They were ready to cooperate with Him in any such work of "reform." Indeed, the people were so forward and so earnest in the matter that they would have actually taken Him by force and made Him King, had He not withdrawn Himself from them. John 6:15. Why, then, did He refuse?

The answer to all this is, Because He was Christ, the Saviour of the world, and had come to help men, not to oppress them; had come to save men, not to destroy them. "The government under which Jesus lived was corrupt and oppressive; on every hand were crying abuses—extortion, intolerance, and grinding cruelty. Yet the Saviour attempted no civil reforms. He attacked no national abuses, nor condemned the national enemies. He did not interfere with the authority or administration of those in power. He who was our Example kept aloof from earthly governments—not because He was indifferent to the woes of men, but because the remedy did not lie in merely human and external measures. To be efficient, the cure must reach men individually and must regenerate the heart.

"Not by the decisions of courts, or councils, or legislative assemblies, not by the patronage of worldly great men, is the kingdom of Christ established; but by the implanting of Christ's nature in humanity through the work of the Holy Spirit. 'As many as received Him, to them gave He power to become the sons of God, even to them that believe on His name; which were born, not of blood, nor of the will of the flesh, nor of the will of man, but of God.' Here is the only power that can work the uplifting of mankind. And the human agency for the accomplishment of this work is the teaching and practising of the Word of God."—*Desire of Ages*, chap. 55, par. 12.

Now Christ is the true Example set by God for every soul in this world to follow. The conduct of Christ is Christianity. Conformity to that Example in the conduct of the individual believer—this and this alone is Christianity in the world. The conduct of Christ, the Example, was totally separate in all things from politics and the affairs of the State. Christianity, therefore, is the total separation of *the believer in Christ* from politics and all the affairs of the State, the total separation of religion and the State *in the individual believer*.

Accordingly, Jesus said to His disciples forever, "Ye are not of the world, but I have chosen you out of the world." John 15:19. And to His Father He said of His disciples forever, "They are not of the world, *even as I* am not of the world." John 17:16. Every Christian in this world, then, must be in the world as Christ was in the world. "As He is, so are we in this world." 1 John 4:17. "It is enough for the disciple that he be as his Master." Matt. 10:25. The Master was always, and in all things, and by fixed design, completely separated from all affairs of politics and the State. And it is forever enough "that the disciple be as his Master."

The following passage from a sermon by the late Thomas Hewlings Stockton presents an infinity of truth, and is worthy to stand forever in letters ablaze with eternal glory:—

"There was one sacrifice too great for Christ to make. He was willing to leave the throne of the universe for the manager of Bethlehem; willing to grow up as the son of a poor carpenter; willing to be called the friend of publicans and sinners; willing to be watched with jealous eyes, and slandered by lying tongues, and hated by murderous hearts, and betrayed by friendly hands, and denied by pledged lips, and rejected by apostate priests and a deluded populace and cowardly princes; willing to be sentenced to the cross, and to carry the cross, and be nailed to the cross, and bleed and groan and thirst and die on the cross. But he was *not* willing to wear an earthly crown or robe, or wield an earthly scepter, or exercise earthly rule. That would have been too great a sacrifice. He did, indeed, endure the crown of thorns and the cast-off purple and the reed, and the cry, 'Hail, King of the Jews!' But this was merely because he preferred the mockery to the reality; so pouring infinite contempt on the one, not only by rejecting it in the beginning of his ministry, but also by accepting the other at its close."

This is the Christianity of Jesus Christ, as respects the great question of religion and the State. And, as in all the instruction from God from the beginning of creation down, it calls always for the complete separation of religion and the State in all things and in all people, in order that the Christian may enjoy infinitely higher things.

"The Powers That Be"

IN the thirteenth and fourteenth chapters of Romans is one of the strongest of the many strong treatises that there are in the Bible upon the total separation of religion and the State—the separation between that which is due to God and that which is due to Cæsar.

First is a recognition of the right of the State to be, and to require subjection and tribute: "Let every soul be subject to the higher powers." "The powers that be are ordained of God." "For this cause pay ye tribute also." "Render therefore to all their dues: tribute to whom tribute is due; custom to whom custom; fear to whom fear; honor to whom honor."

Next is marked the sphere of men's relation to the State: "Owe no man anything, but to love one another; for he that loveth another hath fulfilled the law. For this, Thou shalt not commit adultery, Thou shalt not kill, Thou shalt not steal, Thou shalt not bear false witness, Thou shalt not covet; and if there be any other commandment, it is briefly comprehended in this saying, namely, Thou shalt love thy neighbor as thyself."

Now everybody knows, and Paul knew as well as anybody ever knew, that there are other commandments—other commandments of the very law from which he quoted these. There is the commandment: "Thou shalt have no other gods before Me. Thou shalt not make unto thee any graven image; … thou shalt not bow down thyself to them, nor serve them; for I the Lord thy God am a jealous God, visiting the iniquity of the fathers upon the children unto the third and fourth generation of them that hate Me; and showing mercy unto thousands of them that love Me, and keep My commandments. Thou shalt not take the name of the Lord thy God in vain." "Remember the Sabbath day, to keep it holy. Six days shalt thou labor, and do all thy work; but the seventh day is the Sabbath of the Lord they God; in it thou shalt not do any work; … for in six days the Lord made heaven and earth, the sea, and all that in them is, and rested the seventh day; wherefore the Lord blessed the Sabbath day, and hallowed it."

With these commandments standing as a part, and, indeed, the *first part*, of the very law which he was citing, why did he leave these entirely out and say, "If there be *any other commandment*, it is briefly comprehended in this saying, namely, Thou shalt love thy neighbor as thyself"? Why?—For the simple reason that he was writing of men's relationship and responsibility to *the powers that be, to the State;* and he was laying down the principle that when men have recognized the right of the State to be, have paid the required tribute, and have fulfilled all obligations to their neighbors, there is nothing more for them to render to the State; there is no other commandment in that sphere, and therefore no other duty to be performed toward the powers that be.

This is made certain by the next verse: "Love worketh no ill to his neighbor; therefore love is the fulfilling of the law:" which shows conclusively that it is only the relation of man with man—of man to his neighbor—that is considered in the passage under consideration. The passage is simply an enlargement, an exposition, indeed, of the principle announced by Jesus, "Render to Cæsar the things that are Cæsar's, and to God the things that are God's." When men have recognized the authority of the State, have paid their tribute, and work no ill to their fellow-men, the only relationship or obligation after that is *to God.* The only commandments outside of that sphere are those which mark men's duty towards God.

Thus the Scripture distinctly sets the limit of the jurisdiction or the requirements of the State, at recognition of right to be, tribute, and the relationship of man to man in working no ill to his neighbor. Beyond this the State has no right to go. Outside of this there is nothing for any man to render to the powers that be.

But the Word of the Lord does not stop here; it positively prohibits the powers that be from touching the relationship or obligation of men *to God.*

"Every one of us shall give account of *himself* to God." Rom. 14:12. And that the emphasis is upon the word "*himself*" and not upon the word "account," is certain from the context in the whole chapter. It is not that "every one of us shall give *account* of himself *to God*," nor is it "every one of us shall give account of himself to God." That is all true enough; but that is not the thought expressed in the text.

The one thought particularly expressed is that "every one of us shall give account of *himself* to God." And thus, by the Word of God, all powers that be, all men, and all combinations of men, are positively prohibited from touching, in any way, any man's relationship to God. That rests with man alone; and for his responsibility there, he is to give account *himself* to God.

Again: "One man esteemeth one day above another; another esteemeth every day alike. Let every man be fully persuaded in his own mind. He that regardeth the day, regardeth it unto the Lord; and he that regardeth not the day to the Lord he doth not regard it." Rom. 14:5, 6. The matter of the observance of a day, the duty to esteem one day above another, is not comprehended in that part of the law which relates to neighbors; nor is it comprised in the duties designated as marking the sphere of the powers that be. It is in that part of the law which, by the words "if there be any other commandment, it is briefly comprehended in this saying, namely, thou shalt love thy neighbor as thyself," is definitely excluded from all cognizance of the powers that be.

The observance of a day, the duty to esteem one day above another, is due solely to God. For "he that regardeth the day, regardeth it unto the Lord," not to men. It is comprehended in that part of the law which details man's relationship to God alone, and concerning which to God alone every one is to give account *himself.* Therefore, the powers that be, all men, and all combinations of men, are definitely commanded by the Lord to let every man alone in the matter of the observance of a day. On that subject all are commanded to "let every man be fully persuaded in his own mind." And this because *that* is an obligation due solely to God, and "every one of us shall give account of *himself* to God."

How different are the ways of professed Christians to-day from the Christianity of the New Testament! The vast mass of professed

Christians to-day, in hunting for another commandment in the sphere of the powers that be, would inevitably write it thus: If there be any other commandment, it is briefly comprehended in this saying, namely, Thou shalt do no work on the first day of the week, commonly called Sunday.

But the Christianity of the New Testament, in defining the sphere of the powers that be, says, "If there be any other commandment, it is briefly comprehended in this saying, namely, Thou shalt love thy neighbor as thyself;" and then, as to the observance of a day, commands the powers that be, and all men, and all combinations of men: "Let every man be fully persuaded in his own mind. He that regardeth the day, regardeth it unto the Lord; and he that regardeth not the day to the Lord he doth not regard it." And "every one of us shall give account of himself to God." "Who art thou that judgest another man's servant?"

The day to be esteemed above others is the Sabbath of *the Lord*. "Render therefore ... *to God* the things that are God's." And any man who does not esteem that day above others, who does not regard it unto the Lord, but esteems every day alike, is responsible to God alone and must render account of it *himself* to *God*, and not to man. While the thing that he does is wrong, it is a kind of wrong for which he is responsible to God, and not to the powers that be.

All this also conclusively shows that any movement on the part of the powers that be, or of men or combinations of men *through the powers that be*, to require the observance of a day or to cause men to esteem one day above another, is a plain joining together of what is God's and what is Cæsar's, is a positive union of religion and the State. It is written, "What therefore God hath joined together, let not man put asunder." And by the same token it can be authoritatively written, What God hath put asunder, let no man, nor any combination of men, join together.

Again: This treatise in Romans 13 and 14, on the separation of religion and the State, the separation of what is due to God from what is due to the powers that be, closes with the mighty sentence, "*Whatsoever is not of faith is sin.*"

Whatsoever is of the Word of God is of faith; for faith comes by the Word of God; and "without faith it is impossible to please Him."

Religion is due solely to God; it is "the duty we owe to our Creator, and the manner of discharging it."

Therefore, for the powers that be, or any men *by the powers that be*, to require anything that is *due to God*, is only to subvert faith and require men to sin.

For the powers that be, or any men through the powers that be, to require of any man anything that is due to God, is, in the very act, to unite religion and the State. And as thus to require of men anything that is due to God, is to subvert faith and to require men to sin, it is certain that any connection whatever between religion and the State *is sin*. And, therefore, the greatest example of it that has ever been in the world is aptly and justly designated "the man of *sin*." 2 Thess. 2:3, 4.

And since to "love the Lord thy God with all thy heart, and with all thy soul, and with all thy strength, and with all thy mind; and thy neighbor as thyself"—the keeping of the first two of all the commandments—is complete separation from sin, this brings us again to the truth with which we began,—that the first two of all the commandments, and the keeping of them, are the basis and the surety of the universal and eternal truth of the separation of religion and the State.

Chapter 12

CHRISTIAN PATRIOTISM

WHAT is Christian patriotism in itself?

Patriotism itself is love of country. And the country the love of which is patriotism, is the country of one's birth, or of one's adoption by naturalization.

Christian patriotism, then, being Christian love of country, can be nothing else than the Christian's love of the country of his Christian birth.

But the Christian birth is the new birth; it is the being "born again," which is being "born *from above*." And this "above," the place from which the Christian is born, is *heaven*.

Heaven, then, is the Christian's country. And even so saith the Scripture: "If ye be Christ's, then are ye Abraham's seed, and heirs according to the promise." Gal. 3:29. And to Abraham it was said, "Get thee out of thy country, … into the land that I will show thee." "He … obeyed," and thenceforth he and all his "confessed that they were strangers and pilgrims on the earth. For they that say such things declare plainly that they seek a country. And truly, if they had been mindful of that country from whence they came out, they might have had opportunity to have returned. But now they desire a better country, that is, an *heavenly;* wherefore God is not ashamed to be called their God; for He hath prepared for them a city." Heb. 11:13-16.

Patriotism, then, being love of one's country, and the "heavenly country" being the Christian's country, Christian patriotism is nothing else than love of the heavenly country.

True patriotism is the love of one's country above all other countries: so much so that the true patriot willingly lays down his life for his country. Christian patriotism, then, is the love of the heavenly country above all other countries: so much so that the true Christian will willingly lay down his life for that country.

True patriotism is "the spirit that, originating in love of country, prompts to obedience to its laws; to the support and defense of its existence, rights, and institutions; and to the promotion of its welfare." The Christian's country being only the heavenly country, Christian patriotism is nothing else than the spirit that prompts to obedience to its laws; to the support and defense of its existence, rights, and institutions; and to the promotion of its welfare.

The spirit that, as to the Christian, originates in the love of the Christian's country, is none other than the Holy Spirit. For without being born again, there can be no Christian; and there being no Christian, there can be no love of the Christian's country—no Christian patriotism. Being born again is to be born of the Spirit. Therefore without the Holy Spirit's creating the new creature and the new life, there can be no Christian patriotism.

Are you a Christian patriot? Do you love the Christian's country above all other countries? Have you the spirit that prompts to obedience to the laws of that country, above all other laws; that supports and defends its existence, rights, and institutions above and against those of all other countries?

But may not Christian patriotism, this support and defense of the rights and institutions of the Christian's country, involve fighting?—It not only *may*, but it certainly does. Read: "*Fight* the good fight of *faith*." "The weapons of our warfare are not carnal," yet they are "mighty through God to the pulling down of strongholds; casting down imaginations, and every high thing that exalteth itself against the knowledge of God, and bringing into captivity every thought to the obedience of Christ." 2 Cor. 10:4, 5.

"Wherefore take unto you the whole armor of God, that ye may be able to withstand in the evil day, and having done all, to stand. Stand therefore, having your loins girt about with truth, and having on the breastplate of righteousness; and your feet shod with the preparation of the gospel of peace; above all, taking the shield of faith, wherewith ye shall be able to quench all the fiery darts of the wicked. And take the helmet of salvation, and the sword of the Spirit, which is the Word of God; praying always with all prayer and supplication in the Spirit, and watching thereunto with all perseverance and supplication for all saints." Eph. 6:13-18.

Are you a Christian patriot?

Chapter 13

CHRISTIAN NATURALIZATION

PATRIOTISM is not only love of the country of one's birth, but also love of the country of one's *naturalization*.

Christian patriotism, therefore, is not only love of the country of one's Christian *birth*, but also of one's *Christian naturalization*.

Naturalization is that procedure through which persons born in another country—aliens, foreigners—become citizens of a certain country of their choice.

Is there, then, anything in Christian experience that corresponds to naturalization? Is there such a thing as Christian naturalization? Read Ephesians 2:11: "Wherefore remember, that ye being in time past Gentiles in the flesh, who are called Uncircumcision by that which is called the Circumcision in the flesh made by hands; that *at that time* ye were without Christ, being ALIENS from the commonwealth of Israel, and STRANGERS from the covenants of promise, having no hope, and without God in the world."

Aliens become citizens of a government by naturalization. And when in the act of being naturalized they take the oath of allegiance to the new government, the new sovereign, here are the specifications—copied from a gentleman's certificate of naturalization. You and I were aliens. We have become naturalized into the commonwealth of Israel, the kingdom of God. And now what is involved? Read:—

"This is to certify, etc., that J—B— 'on being admitted to citizenship by this court, took the oath to support the Constitution of the United States of America, and that he then did absolutely and forever renounce and abjure all allegiance and fidelity to every foreign prince, potentate, State, or sovereignty whatsoever, and particularly to the emperor of Germany,' etc., etc."

If he had been a British subject, it would have read, "and particularly to the queen of Great Britain and empress of India."

How much did he have to renounce?—"All allegiance and fidelity to every foreign prince, potentate State, or sovereignty whatsoever." And what in particular?—"And particularly to the emperor of Germany."

And how fully? and for how long?—"*Absolutely* and *forever* renounce and abjure all allegiance and fidelity." Thus he is to turn his back "absolutely" upon all his former "allegiance and fidelity to every foreign prince, potentate, *State*, or *sovereignty* WHATSOEVER." That is in general. And in particular, to the one to whom he was particularly subject. That is, in earthly governments, the way aliens are naturalized.

Now how is it with us, who "were aliens"?—"Now therefore ye are *no more strangers* and *foreigners*, but FELLOW-CITIZENS *with the saints* [not fellow-citizens with *sinners* but "with the saints," Deut. 33:2; Jude 14] and of the household of God; and are built upon the foundation of the apostles and prophets, Jesus Christ Himself being the chief corner-stone." Eph. 2:19, 20. Thank the Lord!

That certificate of naturalization declares that, whatsoever the man may be, he, "on being admitted to citizenship, … did absolutely and forever renounce and abjure all allegiance and fidelity to every foreign prince, potentate, State, or sovereignty whatsoever, and particularly to the" sovereignty to which he had formerly been particularly subject.

In becoming a citizen of the commonwealth of Israel, a fellow-citizen with the saints, did you "absolutely and forever renounce and abjure all allegiance and fidelity to every foreign prince, potentate, State, or sovereignty whatsoever, and *particularly* to the" one to which you were formerly subject, as every alien must do to become a citizen of an earthly government?

If not, then do you count citizenship in the commonwealth of Israel, fellow-citizenship *with the saints*, of as much value as any alien must count citizenship in an earthly government? Do you count fellow-citizenship with the saints of as much value as an alien counts fellow-citizenship with sinners?

In truth and in fact, *is* citizenship in the commonwealth of Israel, is fellow-citizenship with the saints, of as much value as is citizenship in an earthly government, as is fellow-citizenship with sinners?

If citizenship in heaven, if citizenship in the commonwealth of Israel, if fellow-citizenship with the saints, if to be of the household of God, *is indeed* as valuable as is citizenship in an earthly government, then in order to be truly a citizen of the commonwealth of Israel, just as certainly as to be a citizen of an earthly government, it is required that every such one shall "absolutely and forever renounce and abjure all allegiance and fidelity to every foreign prince, potentate, State, or sovereignty whatsoever, and *particularly* to the" one to whom, when an alien, he is subject, which is "the prince of this world."

And if this is not done, what then? If all allegiance to every prince, potentate, state or sovereignty whatsoever, other than that of the commonwealth of Israel, other than that of heaven, other than that of the saints, other than that of the household of God, is not absolutely and forever renounced and abjured, *then* there is certainly attempted a *divided allegiance.*

But will a divided allegiance answer? Will a divided allegiance be accepted? Will any *earthly government* accept a divided allegiance? If any alien asking to become a citizen of an earthly government should refuse to make that renunciation, full and complete as it is; if he should ask to have the renunciation divided, that he might retain and show *some* fidelity, only a little, to some foreign prince, potentate, State, or sovereign; would he be accepted? Everybody knows that he would not, for even a moment. How, then, can it be supposed that such reserved, such *divided,* allegiance could be accepted in any one asking to be a citizen of the commonwealth of Israel?

It is not enough, however, to inquire whether a divided allegiance will be accepted. The true question is, Can there really be *any such thing* as a divided allegiance? And the true answer is, No; for it is written, "No man can serve two masters."

It is therefore certain that no alien, seeking to be a citizen of the commonwealth of Israel, can ever expect to carry with him there any shadow of allegiance to anything *in* this world or *of* this world. It is written: "Love not the world, neither the things that are in the world. If any man love the world, the love of the Father is not in him." 1 John 2:15. Princes, potentates, States, and sovereignties are only of this world. To retain allegiance or fidelity to any of these, is to retain allegiance and fidelity to the things that are only of this world, and, so, to the world itself.

Christian citizenship is citizenship in heaven; for "our citizenship is in heaven." Phil. 3:20. Another translation reads, "For our country [the State to which we belong, of which we by faith are citizens] is in the heavens."—*Alford.* Another, an interlinear, word for word, translation gives it, "For of us the commonwealth in the heavens exists."

Christian citizenship is citizenship in the commonwealth of Israel; for we are no more "aliens from the commonwealth of Israel," "no more strangers and foreigners, but fellow-citizens with the saints, and of the household of God." Eph. 2:12, 13, 18, 19.

Christian patriotism is love of the country of one's citizenship. And true citizenship is the absolute and everlasting renunciation and abjuration of all allegiance and fidelity to every other prince, potentate, State, or sovereignty whatsoever.

Is yours a true Christian citizenship? Are you a Christian patriot?

ADDENDA

Paul's use of Roman citizenship, in which he was born, does not in any sense conflict with the principles of this chapter. For it is to be observed that after he became a Christian, Paul never made any use whatever of that citizenship, nor even mentioned it, except when a prisoner in the hands of the Roman power.

So certainly is this so that he allowed himself to be three times beaten with Roman rods, once to be stoned and dragged out of the city of Lystra, and left for dead, beside many other indignities that could not lawfully be put upon a Roman citizen; and yet nowhere in it all did he so much as mention his Roman citizenship.

But when he was in the hands of the Roman officers and authorities, and they would beat him, as at Jerusalem (Acts 22:25), he said, "Is it lawful for you to scourge a man that is a Roman, and uncondemned?" Or when, held by Cæsar's power at Cæsar's judgment-seat, it was proposed to subject him to the judgment of the

Jews, and this to please the Jews who were clamoring for his life, he said: "I stand at Cæsar's judgment-seat, where I ought to be judged; … no man may deliver me unto them. I appeal unto Cæsar." Acts 25:8-11. Or when he and Silas had been unlawfully beaten and put into prison and in the stocks, and the magistrates sent word to let them go, he returned answer to them, "They have beaten us openly uncondemned, being Romans, and have cast us into prison; and now do they thrust us out privily? nay verily; but let them come themselves and fetch us out." Acts 16:35-37.

Seeing, then, that he never made use nor any mention at all of his Roman citizenship except when he was a prisoner, and then only to insist that the authorities should proceed according to the law which bound *them*, and to the strict observance of which it was perfectly proper that he should hold them, it is evident that what little reference he did make to that citizenship does not conflict with the principle inculcated in his writings, as well as throughout the whole Bible, that the Christian's citizenship is heavenly and not earthly.

Nor does the conduct of either Daniel in Babylon or Joseph in Egypt conflict with the principles here developed from the Scriptures.

Daniel was a captive, and therefore in the condition of a slave, in Babylon. And, though placed in high position and given great responsibility, he was not in any sense a citizen of the kingdom or commonwealth of Babylon, or of Medo-Persia. His patriotism was not in any sense love of the country of Babylon, or of Medo-Persia, but only of Jerusalem, the city of God, and the Lord's holy mountain. Witness his deep anxiety to know when the time would expire and the desolations of Jerusalem be accomplished. Witness his wonderful prayer that God would cause His face to shine upon His sanctuary, and bring His people once more to their beloved Zion. Daniel 9. And witness "his windows being open in his chamber toward Jerusalem," and his prayers there "three times a day." Dan. 6:10. Witness his loyalty to the law and government of God, against those of Babylon and Medo-Persia. He was a *servant* of the kings of Babylon and of Medo-Persia: a highly-honored servant, it is true, yet always only a servant; and even when he was in his most exalted position, he was still referred to as "that Daniel, which is of the children of the captivity of Judah." He served the kings where he was a captive, as he and all his people were commanded by the Lord to do (Jeremiah 29); but through it all he was of those who mournfully chanted:—

"By the rivers of Babylon,
There we sat down, yea, we wept,
When we remembered Zion.
Upon the willows in the midst thereof
We hanged up our harps.
For there they that led us captive required of us songs,
And they that wasted us required of us mirth, saying,
Sing us one of the songs of Zion.
How shall we sing the Lord's song
In a strange land?
If I forget thee, O Jerusalem,
Let my right hand forget her cunning.
Let my tongue cleave to the roof of my mouth,
If I remember thee not;
If I prefer not Jerusalem
Above my chief joy." Psalm 137:1-6, R. V.

It was in principle the same with Joseph. Originally, in Egypt, Joseph was a bought-and-sold slave. And though from prison exalted to the place next to the throne, he was ever only a *servant* of the king of Egypt, and was *never* a *citizen* of Egypt. His patriotism was not love of the country of Egypt, but of the country promised to his fathers, Abraham, Isaac, and Jacob. Witness the impressive fact that he would not allow so much as that even his bones should be buried in Egypt; and his dying and solemn admonition, accepted on oath by his brethren, which was faithfully observed and fulfilled a hundred and forty-four years afterward: "I die; and God will surely visit you, and bring you out of this land unto the land which He sware to Abraham, to Isaac, and to Jacob. And Joseph took an oath of the children of Israel, saying, God will surely visit you, and ye shall carry up my bones from hence." Gen. 50:24, 25; Ex. 13:19; Joshua 24:32.

Thus Daniel and Joseph both being originally slaves in the respective countries of their captivity, their standing and relationships, even in the exalted places to which in the providence of God they were brought, were far different from what these would have been had they been *citizens* of the respective countries where they were. And what they both would have done had the providence of God brought them through such changes as would have given them the standing and relationships of *citizens indeed* of the respective countries where they were,—what then they both would have done, *we know perfectly* from what was actually done by Moses, the great exemplar of their era, and the prototype of the greater Exemplar of our era and of all eras. Moses was in very deed a citizen of Egypt. He was of the royal family, and indisputable heir to the throne. The responsibilities, with the honors, of Egyptian citizenship were upon him, in the fullest sense of the word. But he absolutely and forever renounced and abjured that citizenship, for naturalization in the commonwealth of Israel, for fellow-citizenship with the saints. He left it all, to go with "the people of God." "The reproach of Christ," and even "affliction with the people of God," were to him of far more worth than were all the honors and treasures that attached to Egyptian citizenship.

This being what Moses, the great exemplar of that era, did, and Daniel and Joseph being of the same spirit and character, we know by it precisely what they would have done had they in their respective places been citizens instead of slaves. But, being only servants of the kings where they were, they, like all God-fearing men, were respectful, obedient, and faithful to their "masters according to the flesh."

Chapter 14

THE LAND OF OUR FATHERS

PATRIOTISM is the love of one's country—the country of one's birth—because it is *the land of his fathers.*

Christian patriotism, then, is the love of the country of the Christian's birth, because it is the land of his *Christian* fathers.

The country of the Christian's birth is the heavenly country, because the Christian is born only "from above." The heavenly country, then, is the land of the Christian's fathers.

People are Christians only because they are Christ's people. "And if ye be Christ's, *then* are *ye Abraham's seed,* and *heirs* according to the promise." Gal. 3:29. And the country of our father Abraham was "an heavenly" country only.

Abraham was once a Gentile, was of the nations; but he was born again, was born from above. He was once an alien; but he was naturalized into the kingdom of God, and became a fellow-citizen with the saints.

In becoming naturalized into the kingdom of God, on being admitted into the heavenly citizenship, Abraham was required to get out of his country. Gen. 12:1. This requirement he at once accepted, and he "then did absolutely and forever renounce and abjure all allegiance and fidelity to every foreign prince, potentate, State, or sovereignty whatsoever." He obeyed and went out, "not knowing whither he went," only knowing that he went with God, which was enough for him; and so he became the "father of all them that believe." Rom. 4:11.

When God called Abram out of that country, He also called him into another country, a better, even a heavenly.

Ever after that day, Abraham looked to that country. That is Abraham's country. Wherever he was in *this* world, he was "in a strange country;" and in this strange country he dwelt "in tabernacles with Isaac and Jacob, *the heirs with him* of the *same promise;* for he looked for a city which hath foundations, whose builder and maker is God." And "these all died in faith, not having received the promises, but having seen them afar off, and were persuaded of them, and embraced them, and confessed that they were strangers and pilgrims on the earth. For they that say such things declare plainly that they seek a country. And truly, if they had been mindful of *that country from whence they came out*, they might have had opportunity to have returned. But now they desire a *better country*, that is, AN HEAVENLY; wherefore God is not ashamed to be called their God; for He hath prepared for them a city." Heb. 11:9-16.

We "are all the children of God by faith in Christ Jesus." "And if ye be Christ's, then are ye Abraham's seed, and *heirs* according to the *promise*." As Abraham is the father of all them that believe, and as that heavenly country is Abraham's country, then that heavenly country is the Christian's country. As Christian patriotism is love of the Christian's country, the country of the Christian's fathers; and as *that* country alone is the Christian's country, is the country of the Christian's fathers; so Christian patriotism is love of the country of Abraham, Isaac, Jacob, and CHRIST,—the heavenly country, "the world" of the new earth, the country which God gave in faithful promise to our father.

Are you, now, a true Christian patriot? Is that truly your country? Do you love that country above all other countries that can ever be named or thought of?

And what a country! The wilderness like Eden, and the desert as the garden of the Lord: with only joy and gladness found therein, thanksgiving and the voice of melody. Isa. 51:3. A country where the light of the moon shall be as the light of the sun, and the light of the sun shall be sevenfold, as the light of seven days; and where even then the moon shall be confounded and the sun ashamed in the presence of the glorious Lord who reigns in Mount Zion and in Jerusalem and before His ancients gloriously. Isaiah 30:26; 24:23. A country whose capital city is built all of gold and precious stones and pearls, every several gate of one pearl; a city that has no need of the sun nor the moon to shine in it, because the glory of God lightens it and the Lamb is the light thereof; and the nations of them that are saved shall walk in the light of it, and the gates of it shall not be shut at all by day; for there shall be no night there. Rev. 21:10-25. A country in which the inhabitants shall never say, I am sick; for the people that dwell therein shall be forgiven their iniquity. Isa. 33:24. A country where the people shall all be righteous (Isa. 60:21); and where the wilderness and the solitary place shall be glad for them, and the desert shall rejoice and blossom as the rose; where the eyes of the blind are opened, and the ears of the deaf unstopped; where the lame man shall leap as a hart, and the tongue of the dumb sing; where in the wilderness, waters break out, and streams in the desert; where the ransomed of the Lord shall come to Zion with songs and everlasting joy upon their heads; and where they shall obtain joy and gladness and sorrow and sighing shall flee away." Isa. 35:1-10. A country so quiet and so secure that the people can dwell safely in the wilderness, and sleep in the woods; where the people and the very places round about shall be a blessing; and where there shall be *showers* of blessing. Eze. 34:25, 26. A country where the very land itself shall rejoice even with joy and singing; where for very joy the mountains and the hills shall break forth into singing, and all the trees of the field shall clap their hands. Isa. 55:12. A country in which the tabernacle of God shall be with men, and "He will dwell with them, and they shall be His people, and God Himself shall be with them, and be their God. And God shall wipe away all tears from their eyes; and there shall be no more death, neither sorrow, nor crying, neither shall there be any more pain; for the former things are passed away." Rev. 21:3, 4. A country where "we shall ever feel the freshness of the morning, and shall ever be far from its close."

That is the Christian's country. That is the country of our Christian fathers—of Abraham, our father; of Jesus Christ, the last Adam, and so "the everlasting Father;" and of God, the universal Father, "our Father which art in heaven." Christian patriotism is love of *that* country.

Who would not be a Christian patriot?

Chapter 15

THROUGH THE CHRISTIAN ERA

The book of Revelation in prophetic symbol portrays the fatal consequences, and all history since the book of Revelation was written gives the terrible facts, of the disregard of these principles of divine truth.

There is seen Death, on a pale horse, and Hell following with him, riding forth to kill with sword, and with hunger, and with death, and with the beasts of the earth, souls who were faithful to the Word of God and the testimony which they held. Chap. 6:8-11.

There is seen a great city, "spiritually called Sodom and Egypt," where again "our Lord was crucified." Chap. 11:8.

There is seen a great red dragon persecuting to the death "the woman which brought forth the man child" who "was caught up unto God, and to His throne;" and persecuting "the remnant of her seed, which keep the commandments of God, and have the testimony of Jesus Christ." Chap. 12:13-17.

There is seen a great and dreadful beast in alliance with the dragon, "speaking great things and blasphemies;" opening "his mouth in blasphemy against God, to blaspheme His name, and His tabernacle, and them that dwell in heaven;" making "war with the saints;" exercising his baleful power "over all kindreds, and tongues, and nations," and demanding of them the worship that is due to God only. Chap. 13:1-7.

There is seen an "image of the beast" in alliance with the dragon and the beast, exercising "all the power of the first beast;" deceiving them that dwell on the earth by means of miracles which he had power to do; causing "all, both small and great, rich and poor, free and bond, to receive a mark in their right hand, or in their foreheads; and that no man might buy or sell, save he that had the mark, or the name of the beast, or the number of his name;" and causing "that as many as would not worship the image of the beast should be killed." Chap. 13:11-17.

There is seen a "great whore" "with whom the kings of the earth have committed fornication, and the inhabitants of the earth have been made drunk with the wine of her fornication," sitting "upon a scarlet-colored beast, full of names of blasphemy," the woman "arrayed in purple and scarlet color, and decked with gold and precious stones and pearls, having a golden cup in her hand full of abominations and filthiness of her fornication," upon her forehead a name "written, Mystery, Babylon the Great, the Mother of Harlots and Abominations of the Earth," and she herself "drunken with the blood of the saints, and with the blood of the martyrs of Jesus." Chap. 17:1-6.

Yet over all—death and hell, dragon beast and false prophet, lewd woman and harlot daughters—the saints of God obtain the everlasting victory.

That victory is gained "by the word of God and the testimony which they held," "by the blood of the Lamb and the word of their testimony," by "the everlasting gospel."

Their faithfulness is manifested in keeping the commandments of God and holding the testimony of Jesus Christ (chap. 12:17), by keeping the commandments of God and the faith of Jesus (chap. 14:12).

Therefore upon them is pronounced the divine blessing, and to them there is given the eternal reward: "Blessed are they that do His commandments, that they may have right to the tree of life, and may enter in through the gates into the city." Chap. 22:14. And from the eternal throne goes forth the royal command, "Open ye the gates, that the righteous nation which keepeth the truth may enter in." Isa. 26:2.

"And I saw as it were a sea of glass mingled with fire; and them that had gotten the victory over the beast, and over his image, and over his mark, and over the number of his name, stand on the sea of glass, having the harps of God. And they sing the song of Moses the servant of God, and the song of the Lamb, saying, Great and marvelous are Thy works, Lord God Almighty; just and true are Thy ways, thou King of saints. Who shall not fear Thee, O Lord, and glorify Thy name? for Thou only art holy; for all nations shall come and worship before Thee; for Thy judgments are made manifest." Chap. 15:2-4.

"And I saw thrones, and they that sat upon them; and judgment was given unto them; and I saw the souls of them that were beheaded for the witness of Jesus, and for the word of God, and which had not worshiped the beast, neither his image, neither had received his mark upon their foreheads, or in their hands; and they lived and reigned with Christ a thousand years."

"And I saw a new heaven and a new earth; for the first heaven and the first earth were passed away; and there was no more sea. And I John saw the holy city, New Jerusalem, coming down from God out of heaven, prepared as a bride adorned for her husband. And I heard a great voice out of heaven saying, Behold, the tabernacle of God is with men, and He will dwell with them, and they shall be His people, and God Himself shall be with them, and be their God. And God shall wipe away all tears from their eyes; and there shall be no more death, neither sorrow, nor crying, neither shall there be any more pain; for the former things are passed away."

"And there shall be no more curse; but the throne of God and of the Lamb shall be in it; and His servants shall serve Him; and they shall see His face; and His name shall be in their foreheads. And there shall be no night there; and they need no candle, neither light of the sun; for the Lord God giveth them light; and

"THEY SHALL REIGN FOREVER AND EVER."

Thus is vindicated the loyalty of men to Christian principle; and this is the reward of Christian patriotism.

CHRISTIAN LOYALTY

EVERYTHING that the Lord has ever done for mankind since the sin of Adam, has been done solely to bring man back into harmony with His law.

The establishment of ordinances; the giving of His law; the sending of His prophets; the sending of His Son, "that Prophet" greater than all; the gift of His Holy Spirit; and the gifts of the Spirit—all, everything, that has been given, established, or employed by the Lord, has been to bring men to obedience to His law.

In bringing men to His law He is bringing them to Himself; for it is written: Thou "testifiedst against them, that Thou mightest bring them again unto *Thy law*," and "testified against them to turn them *to Thee*." Neh. 9:29, 26. Read carefully the whole chapter, and see the object of all that He did. Bringing men to His law is only turning them to Himself; because "God is love," and this is the love of God, that we keep His commandments."

No higher attainment than the love of God can ever be reached by any soul in the wide universe. And since it is the love of God, and only the love of God, "that we keep His commandments," it is the very certainty of truth that no higher attainment than the keeping of the commandments of God can ever be reached by any soul in the wide universe.

Jesus said, "I have kept My Father's commandments, and abide in His love," and "I and My Father are one." There can not possibly be any higher nor any better attainment than *oneness* with God: than likeness to Christ, who is one with God. And as He kept the Father's commandments and abode in His love, and abode in His love by keeping His commandments, so there is no higher nor better thing that could possibly be attainable than the keeping of the commandments of God.

The greatest gift of God to men is the gift of His only-begotten Son, Jesus Christ. Yet with this wondrous gift to men, even in Christ nothing avails on the part of men "but faith which worketh by love." Faith is the gift of God, and, working by love, works only by the love of God. And "this is the love of God, that we keep His commandments." Therefore it is certain that the one great object of the very gift of Christ, and of faith in Him, is to bring men to the keeping of the commandments of God, to faithful obedience to His law.

The greatest gift God can bestow on men through Jesus Christ, the only means of this gift to men, is His Holy Spirit. Yet in this gift all that He does, all that He can do, is to cause men to know the love of God: for "the love of God is shed abroad in our hearts by the Holy Ghost which is given unto us." Rom. 5:5.

And since it is "the love of God, that we keep His commandments," and "love is the fulfilling of the law," it is perfectly plain that the one purpose of this greatest gift of God through Christ is the keeping of the commandments of God, faithful allegiance to His law.

All the working of the Spirit of God, through all the diversities of operations, is to bring souls unto charity, the bond of perfectness, which is perfect love, the love of God. And "this is the love of God, that we keep His commandments." Therefore all the working of the Spirit of God, through His many gifts and operations, is solely to bring men to the keeping of the commandments of God.

By all this therefore it is certain that the keeping of the commandments of God is the greatest blessing, the highest honor, and the richest gift that even God can bestow upon any soul. All other blessings honors, and gifts are subordinate to this; they are given only to be conducive to this one thing; and they are to be used only as means of attaining this.

For any person to use any of the gifts of God for any other purpose than to make himself a true keeper of the commandments of God, is for that person to miss the will of God, and to frustrate the object of the very gift which he would use. To be willing to use the Word of God, to use God's gift of His dear Son, to use the gift of the Holy Spirit, or any of the gifts of the Holy Spirit, with any other aim than the perfect keeping of the commandments of God, is to miss the will of God, and to pervert the purpose of that Word, or that gift. That one aim, and that alone, is true Christianity.

This is what *Christian patriotism* means. So to honor the law of God is what it means to be a true citizen of the commonwealth of Israel. This is what means loyalty to the government of God, and allegiance to the constitution the supreme law of the Most High.

Now are you a Christian patriot? Is the keeping of the commandments of God your one single aim? Are all the gifts and blessings of God counted by you as only contributory to this one single object? These questions are important. This whole subject, as here presented, is of vital importance to every soul; for the loyalty of every soul to God, to His government, to His law, is to be tested to the uttermost in this time, when "the hour of His judgment is come," and when, of all who shall stand in the judgment and be saved, it is declared from heaven, "Here are they that keep the commandments of God, and the faith of Jesus." Rev. 14:6-12.

Here are the commandments of God, His holy law:

"I AM THE LORD THY GOD, WHICH HAVE BROUGHT THEE OUT OF THE LAND OF EGYPT, AND OUT OF THE HOUSE OF BONDAGE.

"THOU SHALT HAVE NO OTHER GODS BEFORE ME.

"THOU SHALT NOT MAKE UNTO THEE ANY GRAVEN IMAGE, OR ANY LIKENESS OF ANYTHING THAT IS IN HEAVEN ABOVE, OR THAT IS IN THE EARTH BENEATH, OR THAT IS IN THE WATER UNDER THE EARTH; THOU SHALT NOT BOW DOWN THYSELF TO THEM, NOR SERVE THEM; FOR I THE LORD THY GOD AM A JEALOUS GOD, VISITING THE INIQUITY OF THE FATHERS UPON THE CHILDREN UNTO THE THIRD AND FOURTH GENERATION OF THEM THAT HATE ME; AND SHOWING MERCY UNTO THOUSANDS OF THEM THAT LOVE ME, AND KEEP MY COMMANDMENTS.

"THOU SHALT NOT TAKE THE NAME OF THE LORD THY GOD IN VAIN; FOR THE LORD WILL NOT HOLD HIM GUILTLESS THAT TAKETH HIS NAME IN VAIN.

"REMEMBER THE SABBATH DAY, TO KEEP IT HOLY. SIX DAYS SHALT THOU LABOR, AND DO ALL THY WORK; BUT THE SEVENTH

DAY IS THE SABBATH OF THE LORD THY GOD; IN IT THOU SHALT NOT DO ANY WORK, THOU, NOR THY SON, NOR THY DAUGHTER; THY MAN SERVANT, NOR THY MAID SERVANT, NOR THY CATTLE, NOR THY STRANGER THAT IS WITHIN THY GATES; FOR IN SIX DAYS THE LORD MADE HEAVEN AND EARTH, THE SEA, AND ALL THAT IN THEM IS, AND RESTED THE SEVENTH DAY; WHEREFORE THE LORD BLESSED THE SABBATH DAY, AND HALLOWED IT.

"HONOR THY FATHER AND THY MOTHER; THAT THY DAYS MAY BE LONG UPON THE LAND WHICH THE LORD THY GOD GIVETH THEE.

"THOU SHALT NOT KILL.

"THOU SHALT NOT COMMIT ADULTERY.

"THOU SHALT NOT STEAL.

"THOU SHALT NOT BEAR FALSE WITNESS AGAINST THY NEIGHBOR.

"THOU SHALT NOT COVET THY NEIGHBOR'S HOUSE, THOU SHALT NOT COVET THY NEIGHBOR'S WIFE, NOR HIS MAN SERVANT, NOR HIS MAID SERVANT, NOR HIS OX, NOR HIS ASS, NOR ANYTHING THAT IS THY NEIGHBOR'S."

These commandments are summed up in the following *two;* because "on these two commandments hang all the law and the prophets":—

"Hear, O Israel: The Lord our God is one Lord; and thou shalt love the Lord thy God with all thy heart, and with all thy soul, and with all thy mind, and with all thy strength."

"Thou shalt love thy neighbor as thyself."

This alone is Christian patriotism; and Christian patriotism is, in every individual who possesses it, the total separation of religion and the State.